MOZART

Decorations by Warren Chappell

MANUEL KOMROFF

MOZART

NEW YORK

Alfred · A · Knopf

1956

L. C. catalog card number: 56–5273

© MANUEL KOMROFF, 1956

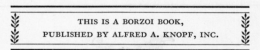

THIS IS A BORZOI BOOK,
PUBLISHED BY ALFRED A. KNOPF, INC.

FIRST EDITION

CONTENTS

I · *The Birth of a Golden Spirit* 3
II · *The Wonder Children* 18
III · *The Grand Tour* 26
IV · *Salzburg and Vienna* 48
V · *The Italian Tour* 63
VI · *Work, Bondage, and the Dream of Freedom* 73
VII · *The Last Grand Tour* 81
VIII · *Paris* 89
IX · *Romance* 98
X · *The Break for Freedom* 102
XI · *Vienna and Marriage* 109
XII · Figaro *and Prague* 126
XIII · *The Full Flowering* 135
XIV · *The Closing Year* 153
XV · *And After* 167
· *A Note about the Köchel Listing* 170
· *Index* *follows page* 171

v

ILLUSTRATIONS

[FOLLOWING PAGE 86]

View of the town and citadel of Salzburg, 1795.
Photograph of Mozart's birthplace.
Anna Maria Mozart, the composer's mother.
Leopold Mozart, the composer's father.
Mozart at the age of six.
Mozart's sister, Nannerl, at the age of eleven.
Autograph manuscript of the Minuet in G (K.1).
Leopold, Wolfgang, and Nannerl at Paris.
Mozart at about the age of thirteen.
Mozart at the age of twenty-one.
The Mozart family at Salzburg.
Constanze Mozart.
Mozart, about 1783.
Hieronymous Colloredo.
Joseph II.
Emanuel Schikaneder.

vii

Lorenzo da Ponte.

First page of the autograph score of the Requiem (K.626).

Letter from Mozart to his wife.

The last authentic portrait of Mozart.

Mozart monument at Vienna.

MOZART

The Birth of a Golden Spirit

Mozart was born on the night of January 27, 1756. At ten o'clock the next morning his father wrapped the new born infant in a warm blanket and carried him down the three flights of stone steps that led from their modest apartment. Then he hurried as fast as he could through the winding streets of old Salzburg to the Cathedral.

Here a priest baptized the child. The town chaplain opened his large baptismal register and, dipping his quill pen in the ink, recorded the fact that a boy child had been born to the honorable Herr Leopold Mozart, court musician, and Anna Maria his wife. Then dipping his quill again he paused and asked: "And what do you name him?"

"Let him be called Joannes Chrysostomus Wolfgang Gottlieb Mozart."

Such a long name for a tiny baby! The "Gottlieb" meant "beloved of God," but the town chaplain actually wrote the Greek form of the word, "Theophilus," into the baptismal register. A few years later the family began to use the Latin form of this same name, "Amadeus," and the child eventually became known as Wolfgang Amadeus Mozart.

As soon as the town chaplain had inscribed the long imposing name in the baptismal register, the father hurried home with his precious bundle. The January wind was bitter cold, and he walked as fast as he could crossing the Cathedral square, hurrying past the palace of his patron, the Archbishop of Salzburg.

Salzburg is situated in western Austria, close to the German border and about a hundred miles north of Italy. Because of this it is a sort of in-between place that is not quite Austrian, German, or Italian, but is influenced by each of these lands.

The city of Salzburg and its province were in ancient times inhabited by Celts who were conquered by the Romans. After the Middle Ages this city and province were governed by independent and powerful Roman Catholic archbishops, who ruled like kings. The country about was rich in minerals and salt mines from which they derived great revenues.

Just before 1600, a prince-bishop, who was related

4

to the famous Medici family, was elected to rule over Salzburg. When he arrived in this ancient town, with its dark narrow winding streets, and visited the great fortress castle on the hill where he was supposed to live, he was horrified. "What barbarism!" he cried. Inspired by the Italian Renaissance and the great architecture of Rome, he tore down many of the old dark churches and medieval houses. He straightened many of the streets, enlarged the square, and built a palace for himself, monasteries for his monks, fine stables for his horses, and many beautiful gardens. Then he sent to Italy for one of the best architects and ordered him to make plans for a cathedral which, though smaller in scale, should resemble St. Peter's in Rome.

So it was that the town of Salzburg, nestled in the beautiful hills of the Austrian Tyrol which roll southward to form the lofty Alps, was transformed into a little jewel city. So it was that the powerful Italian prince-bishop prepared a fitting setting for the birth, a century and a half later, of Mozart, one of the world's greatest musicians.

Mozart was more than a musical genius. Mozart was a miracle. He lived only thirty-five years. His brief life was spent in constant struggle. Europe was his battleground and kings and queens his audience. He died in want. Yet he left behind him a vast musical empire and we are his heirs.

His story is the story of the soul of an artist struggling against poverty, ill-health, misfortune, and lack of appreciation. However, never for an instant did his courageous spirit abandon him. Not a single line of his music falls into despair or sounds a morbid strain. It is ever soaring above the world with nobility of spirit and courage.

It seems as though Mozart came to us directly from heaven to enrich our world, and then flew back again. While he was here he poured out his heart in fleeting melody and lent his golden wings to give flight to his music. Before his short visit was ended he had created over a thousand compositions. This is our heritage, a whole empire of music that has in it the golden glow of a sun god.

Mozart's father, Leopold Mozart, was born in Augsburg, in southern Germany not far from Munich. Here the Mozart family can be traced back for many generations. They spelled their name Mozert, Motzhardt, and Motard.

Leopold Mozart's great-grandfather, his grandfather and his father were bookbinders. Leopold was the first in the family to become a musician, but this he did not achieve without protest. As a child he taught himself to play the violin. However, his father, the bookbinder, was determined that the boy should become a priest and Leopold was therefore given religious training. He served several years in the choir of a monastery where he acquired a taste for church music and was allowed to practice on the organ. But religious training did not suit his nature and when he was eighteen years old he entered the university of Salzburg, where for about a year he studied logic and law. Logic and law did not satisfy his nature any better than religion and finally, completely disregarding his father's wishes, he decided to make music his career.

After leaving the university, Leopold Mozart entered the service of a local count as a combination valet and musician. A few years later, at the age of twenty-four, he was offered the position of fourth violinist in the private orchestra of the Archbishop of Salzburg, Count von Schrattenbach.

The Archbishop's orchestra consisted of thirty-three musicians. This number was enlarged for special occasions by the addition of court trumpeters and town musicians as well as thirty adult singers and fifteen young choirboys.

It was Leopold's duty to teach these choirboys to play the violin. Some years later, at the death of the Cathedral organist, he was also called upon to teach the clavier, which was the forerunner of our present-day piano. Leopold Mozart was an accomplished composer, and it was his further duty to see that the Cathedral had suitable music for its various services. For all these labors Leopold was paid four hundred gulden a year, or about seven hundred and fifty dollars

7

in our money. This was just enough to keep body and soul together.

When Leopold was twenty-eight he married a very pretty girl named Anna Maria Pertl. They were considered a very handsome couple and one of the happiest in all Salzburg. Their characters seemed to complement each other. Leopold was stern, serious, and often pompous and pessimistic. Anna Maria, on the other hand, loved gaiety and was rarely serious. She was neither very well educated nor over-intelligent, but she had a generous heart, a pleasant, easy-going nature, and made an excellent housekeeper. She had no artistic temperament whatsoever, and was not over-sensitive. But her good heart and her genial, happy nature made her a devoted wife and a splendid mother for her two children.

Both these children were born in a poor little apartment up three stone flights in an old Salzburg building. Because of Mozart's great musical genius this building has been preserved and is now a museum. The room where Wolfgang Mozart was born may be seen today by visitors to Salzburg.

The first child born to Leopold and Anna Maria was a little girl named Maria Anna or Marianne. But with typical Salzburg familiarity she was soon called Nannerl, and this affectionate nickname remained with her all her life.

Four and a half years later Wolfgang was born. The innocent infant, who through his genius was destined to make the name Mozart known throughout the world, was at once weighed down with that very long and high-sounding name which his proud father dictated to the town chaplain—Joannes Chrysostomus Wolfgang Gottlieb Mozart.

From the very first day of his life, as he lay in his cradle, he listened to music. It was impossible not to hear it. The bedroom was close to the living-room where every day his father practiced on the violin and piano and also gave private music lessons to Salzburg children. The infant Mozart woke up to music and fell asleep to music. When he drank his milk he heard strains of music. The air he breathed was ever filled with fleeting sound.

With music he grew. Even before he could speak his parents noticed that he seemed to know when a note was flat or sharp and when the notes of a chord were pleasant or dissonant. Concords seemed to please him. Noisy and sour discords disturbed him.

As soon as the child was able to walk, he went to the piano and touched the keys. Unlike most children who slap the keyboard and enjoy the noise, little Mozart pressed each of the keys gently and listened to the clear tones. When he was about three, he discovered that thirds were very pleasing and with two little fingers he tried the thirds up and down the keyboard. He smiled. He was happy.

9

Mozart's sister Nannerl also displayed a talent for music, and while she was still very young her father began to give her lessons on the clavier. These lessons made a great impression on little Mozart. Instead of playing with his toys like other very small children, he listened to every word that was said and to every note that was played. Sometimes he tried to pick out the melody he had heard his sister practice. Then, turning to his father, he would beg to be given lessons.

"He is still too young," his mother would say.

But Papa Mozart would smile and place his son's little fingers on the keyboard. At first, only in fun, he showed him how to hold his hands and how to press the keys. Then soon, very soon, without effort, Wolfgang was able to play with both hands correctly and in perfect time. By the time he reached the age of four he was already playing simple pieces and easy minuets.

The first book of music from which little Mozart studied was a special volume his father had put together to teach Nannerl. This volume contained simple pieces, minuets and exercises in various keys and tempos, written by composers of the day, some of whom were friends of Leopold Mozart.

The book began with the easiest compositions, written in the simplest keys, and went on to the more difficult pieces. Each piece was a little harder than the previous one.

This volume has been preserved and we can read some of the father's notations. In the margin of the eighth minuet Leopold Mozart wrote: "This minuet was learned by little Wolfgang in his fourth year." In another place, beside a more difficult page, we read: "This minuet and trio little Wolfgang learned in half-an-hour at half past nine o'clock on January 26, 1761, one day before his fifth birthday."

The child could learn a new page of music in half-an-hour! And after playing it over only a few times he knew it by heart and could later play it from memory.

In his fifth year, Mozart began to compose little pieces of his own. He still did not know how to write musical notes on paper, but he played his pieces on the keyboard and his father took them down for him. In this way were his first compositions recorded.

But this method did not satisfy the child. He watched carefully to see how musical notes were written and secretly, when he was alone, he took the pen and ink-bottle and tried to do what he had so often seen his father do.

He was still in his fifth year when one day his father came home with a good friend named Schachtner, a court trumpeter. As they entered they saw little Wolfgang sitting at a table and dipping a pen to the bottom of an inkwell. Each time he brought up a full load of ink which quickly blotted on the page before him, but the boy wiped the blots away with the back of his hand and managed somehow to mark notes on the paper.

"What are you doing?" asked his father.

"I am writing a concerto. It will soon be done."

"Let me see it."

"It's not finished yet."

"Never mind. Let me see it. I am sure it must be very fine."

His father lifted a sheet of the smeared music paper and showed it to his friend Schachtner. It was a very messy page filled with smudge blots over which many notes and other musical notations were written. At first they laughed, for it seemed like musical nonsense. But after examining the page carefully Leopold began to notice that the notes made sense.

"Look, Herr Schachtner," he said with tears of pride in his eyes, "see how correct and orderly it is. Only it can never be played because it is too complicated and too difficult!"

"That is why it is a concerto," said little Wolfgang seriously. "It must be practiced until it is learned. Look! This is how it goes."

He went to the keyboard and tried to play what he had written on the paper. His hands were too small and could not reach all the notes, but he managed with the melody and tempo to show what he had intended to compose. And he also illustrated which parts were to be carried by the piano and which by the orchestra.

He was five years old. He did not know how to hold a pen or dip it properly into an inkwell. He could not even write his name. Yet with blots and smudges he had attempted to write a difficult musical composition with correct harmonies and interesting rhythms!

Leopold and Anna Mozart were naturally very proud of their little son. Such talent, they felt, bordered on genius that could only have come from heaven. They were also very proud of Nannerl, for she too was extremely talented. Leopold was eager that under his guidance his children should develop their natural musical gifts and gain technical perfection.

It was to this end that he worked. And it was not long before little Wolfgang and Nannerl became justly known in Salzburg as the "wonder children."

As a music teacher Leopold Mozart was methodical and thorough. He not only knew the theory of music but also had had experience in teaching composition, the violin, the piano, and the organ. As a composer he turned out work that compared favorably with that of the average musician of his day. It was not brilliant or very original, nor was it inspired, but it was correct and workmanlike. He wrote some serious music, symphonies and quartets, but he was better known for light descriptive music which pictured peasants' weddings, hunts, sleigh-parties, soldiers marching with fife and drums, and galloping horses.

He tried to describe the daily life of the ordinary people.

In the year that his son Wolfgang was born, Leopold Mozart wrote and published a book on violin playing that soon made him well known in the musical world. His *Violin Method* was at once recognized as an important contribution to the subject. It was translated into several languages, enjoyed a wide circulation, and for many years was considered one of the standard works on violin playing.

From this work we learn that Leopold Mozart was a careful, methodical, and strict teacher. He believed in hard work and much practice. He also warned music teachers not to try to advance their pupils too rapidly, but rather to be patient and wait for the right time. This was good advice.

However, Leopold Mozart was not always so wise in his teaching. He made some exercises in this book purposely distasteful, believing that young people should not be pampered, but should learn to do things that are disagreeable. This he felt was part of musical education and important for character development.

Through these instructions, and also from the many letters which have been preserved, we are to-day able to draw a true picture of Leopold's qualities and defects. He was a man of ability, conservative, home-loving, devoted to his wife and children, hard-working, respectful of his superiors, and very sane and practical. On the other hand he lacked imagination and he was completely humorless. He was strict, even severe. He was cool and calculating, very critical of the faults of others, bitter and sarcastic. He complained a great deal, was distrustful and ambitious.

Leopold Mozart could have written a piano-method volume as well as one for the church organ. But his duties as court violinist and music teacher did not leave him much free time. He did, however, compile two volumes for his children. The first book, from which Mozart received his earliest instruction, had been written for Nannerl. The second, which was more advanced, was ready for Wolfgang's sixth birthday. It was inscribed as a present "to my dear son," and consisted of one hundred and thirty-five pages of all types of music, old and new, with examples that included all the keys, even the most difficult.

Little Wolfgang received another present during his sixth year. One of his father's friends gave him a violin, the very smallest size made. The child was delighted, and begged his father to give him lessons. But Leopold refused. "You are still too young," he said. "And besides, the piano practice and your lessons in harmony are enough to fill your time."

But little Mozart could not be brushed aside. When

he was alone he would take out his small violin, tune the strings, and try to pick out a melody. All this he did by himself out of sheer curiosity.

One afternoon his father came home with his friend Schachtner, the court trumpeter, and another musician whose name was Wenzel. These three had planned to spend the afternoon playing some new trios which had recently been sent to them. Papa Mozart was to play bass, Wenzel first violin, and Schachtner second violin. Just when they were ready to start, little Wolfgang ran into the room, and seeing what was going on, begged to be allowed to play second violin. He ran off and brought out his little fiddle.

His father said: "How can you expect to play when you have never had a lesson on the violin?"

"One need not have learned in order to play second violin," the child answered.

At this they all laughed. But little Mozart was serious.

Then his father grew irritated and told him to go away and not to make a nuisance of himself. Wolfgang began to cry. And at length Schachtner interceded on his behalf.

"All right," said Papa Mozart. "You can play with Herr Schachtner, but play so softly that we do not hear your sour notes."

The boy brushed away his tears and took his place at the music stand. They began to play.

Schachtner was soon astonished to hear that Wolf-gang was playing in perfect tune and rhythm. He put his violin down. Wolfgang continued playing, and Papa Mozart could hardly see the notes on the page before him, for tears had filled his eyes.

When they came to the end of the trio, the three men applauded and praised little Mozart. The child was so pleased and encouraged that he boasted: "I could even play the part of the first violin at sight."

They all laughed again.

"I could. I could," he insisted.

And just for a joke they let him try. He made a bold attempt. Here and there he did manage to carry the melody, but in many places the music was too difficult for him.

However, all agreed that for his first time, without having had a single lesson, he did very well. Wonderfully well! And after this his father consented to give him lessons on the violin in addition to his lessons on the piano and his lessons in composition.

The Wonder Children

Leopold Mozart was very proud of his "wonder children" and he wanted to display them before the world. Salzburg was such a small and unimportant place. He wanted all Europe to see and hear Wolfgang and Nannerl. Besides, by presenting his children before the aristocracy and the crowned heads of Europe he was certain he could make a little extra money for the family. The salary he received from the Archbishop was very small and provided for only the barest necessities. The family was often in debt. Extra money would be welcome. He decided to take his son and daughter on a tour.

To carry out this plan, Leopold Mozart obtained a leave of absence from the Archbishop. Then one day, leaving Mamma Mozart at home, he took the children for a long coach ride to Munich, the Bavarian capital.

Munich was only a hundred miles away, but in those days a hundred miles was quite a distance. Nevertheless, the children enjoyed riding in the coach. It was an adventure. They enjoyed looking out of the window and watching the landscape, which was ever moving, ever changing. They enjoyed the crunching wheels, the swaying coach, the crack of the coachman's whip, and the gay sound of the horses' running hoofs.

This was little Wolfgang's and Nannerl's first long coach ride. At the time they did not know that a great part of their young lives would be spent riding together in coaches to and from Europe's great capitals. They did not know that this first trip would lead to many others.

Arriving in Munich, Papa Mozart succeeded in gaining an audience with the Elector of Bavaria, Maximilian Joseph. The Mozart children played for this important man, Wolfgang performing a concerto. The Elector, who was himself an excellent violoncellist, received them kindly, and expressed great admiration. After three weeks Leopold and the children returned to Salzburg.

Encouraged by this initial success, Papa Mozart began to plan another trip. He hoped to make a longer journey and visit Vienna, the capital of Austria. He knew that the Empress Maria Theresa and the Emperor Francis I were both fond of music. The Empress sang very well and all her children, including Marie Antoinette who was about the same age as Wolfgang, had musical training. This time Leopold was certain he would not be confronted by a barrier of ignorance.

Although Vienna at that time had not yet reached its great musical glory—the glory that was ushered in a generation later with Beethoven and Schubert—it was already almost as famous a musical center as Paris or London. It was to this place that Leopold Mozart planned to bring his "wonder children." Here he was certain their great talents would be appreciated. The best time for the visit, he knew, would be in the fall of the year, when the nobility returned from their country estates. And so he waited for the summer to pass. He waited and he planned.

In September of that same year, the year Wolfgang was six, Leopold Mozart got another leave of absence from the Archbishop of Salzburg, borrowed some money from his landlord, Lorenz Hagenauer who was also his friend, and hired a coach to take the whole family, including Mamma Mozart, to Vienna. On top of the coach were tied a small clavier, two violins, a case of music, and their boxes of clothes.

Traveling by private coach was a great luxury, but Papa Mozart wanted everyone to know that his children were very superior. He was proud of their unusual accomplishments and, since he was courting royal patronage, he was anxious to play the game and arrive in style.

The Mozarts broke the journey at Passau, where the local bishop was eager to hear Wolfgang perform. Like Maximilian Joseph, the bishop understood a good deal about music. He was so charmed with little Mozart that he detained the family in Passau for five days so that he could hear the child play several times. But the good bishop was very economical. In the end he rewarded Papa Mozart with a single ducat, a small gold coin worth about two dollars. This was very disappointing, but Papa Mozart hoped for better fortune in the future.

On the way to Vienna the Mozarts made another stop, this time at a monastery where little Wolfgang was allowed to try the big organ. The monks were at supper, but as soon as they heard the wonderful music they left their tables and came into the chapel to see who it was that was playing.

"It is only a boy!" exclaimed one.

"Yes, a boy," said another. "But that boy is Mozart, one of the wonder children of Salzburg!"

The fame of the Mozart children was beginning to spread.

After resting in the monastery, the Mozarts went on, but before reaching Vienna the coach was halted by customs inspectors.

Little Wolfgang was very friendly with the customs officers and spoke to them as though he had known them all his life. He was far from being shy.

"My sister and I play the clavier which is on top of the coach, and I also play the violin. The little one is mine. The big one is Papa's. We are going to Vienna to play for the Empress!"

The officers smiled as though they did not believe a single word the boy was saying.

He took out his little fiddle, lifted the bow, and played a minuet.

"Now do you believe me?" he asked when he was through.

As a result, the customs officials passed all the Mozart family baggage without inspection and without payment, and the coach rolled on to Vienna.

The fame of the "wonder children" from Salzburg had gone before them. Vienna welcomed them with open arms.

At last Papa Mozart found appreciation for his talented boy and girl. Fame and fortune, he was sure, would soon follow.

To Hagenauer back home he wrote most enthusiastically: "Today we were at the French Ambassador's, and tomorrow we shall go to Count Harrach's. We are everywhere brought and sent back in the carriages of the nobility. We have agreed to be present from six to nine o'clock at a grand concert, in which all the greatest artists of Vienna will perform. . . . On one occasion we were at a house from half-past two until near four o'clock; then Count Hardegg sent his carriage for us, which took us full gallop to the house of a lady, where we stayed until half-past five; afterwards we were with Count Kauniz until near nine. . . . Everywhere the ladies are in love with my boy."

And so it was that the Mozart children from sleepy little Salzburg were plunged into the busy life and big world of the nobility in Vienna. They were received in the most dazzling homes and palaces, climbed marble stairways lined with footmen in livery, and walked across highly polished parquet floors. Such wealth, such splendor! It was all like a dream.

And then, after many days, the moment which Papa Mozart had hoped for suddenly arrived. His "wonder children" were invited to appear at the Royal Palace.

For three long hours they were with the Emperor and Empress. During this time Wolfgang played on the piano together with his sister and also alone. Then he played his little violin while she accompanied him at the keyboard. There was a great deal of applause and much praise, and little Wolfgang was so happy that impulsively he ran to the Empress, climbed up on her lap, put his arms about her neck, and kissed her. So spontaneous and natural was his manner that the entire court was charmed.

The next day the Empress Maria Theresa sent Papa Mozart one hundred gold ducats as well as a beautiful dress for Nannerl and a suit for Wolfgang. There was also an invitation to return to the palace for another concert.

The suit which the Empress gave little Wolfgang was made of the finest lilac-colored cloth. The waistcoat was of the same color, only of silk embroidered all over with leaves and flowers. Both coat and waistcoat were edged with a broad band of gold embroidery, and since this suit had originally been made for a royal prince it had a little sword. Nannerl's dress was just as elegant. It was the court dress of one of the young princesses and was made of white brocaded taffeta with fine lace and embroidery.

Dressed like a prince and a princess, the Mozart children returned to the Royal Palace for their second concert. On this day, too, they played so beautifully that everyone was again charmed. The Emperor Francis called Wolfgang a little magician after the boy had shown how he could play the clavier even when the keys were covered with a light cloth.

After this Leopold and Anna's "wonder children" came to the palace each day to perform for the royal family and their guests. They were so well liked that they were soon playing and running about the palace corridors with the royal children.

One day when they were all running down a long hall Wolfgang slipped on the highly polished floor. The young Archduchess Marie Antoinette, who was then seven years old, helped him to his feet.

"You are very kind," said little Mozart. "Some day I will marry you."

The Empress later asked Wolfgang why he had said that. He replied: "Out of gratitude. She was good to me, but her sister stood by and did not help me."

This was the same Marie Antoinette who later became the unfortunate Queen of France and ended her life on the scaffold of the Revolution.

The happy days in Vienna, however, suddenly ended. Little Wolfgang fell sick with scarlet fever and though his case was not too serious it was four full weeks before he could be moved and before the homeward journey could be undertaken. During this time much of the profit gained by the successful visit was used up for medical care and living expenses.

In spite of all this, Papa Mozart was pleased. In Vienna the Mozarts had enjoyed a taste of real glory. He plotted grand schemes for the future. His ambition drove him on. Vienna, he felt, was only the beginning. There would be other days, greater successes, more applause, real wealth!

1763   1766

The Grand Tour

Encouraged by the great success Wolfgang and Nannerl had achieved in Vienna, Leopold Mozart now plunged his children into serious work. He insisted that they practice long hours every day. Their keyboard exercises grew more difficult and more complicated week by week.

Papa Mozart knew that his son and daughter must continue to develop musically if this first success was to be followed by the future triumphs he hoped for. He devoted every moment he could spare to the children's musical education. The result was that by the age of twelve Nannerl performed at the keyboard with all the confidence of a mature musician and the seven-year-old Wolfgang not only rivaled his sister at the piano but also played the violin and composed original music.

Papa Mozart was not satisfied. He wanted his children to be more than accomplished musicians. He wanted them to be concert virtuosos. He wanted them to become the sensation of Europe. And it was to this end that he devised more and more exercises for their musical training.

All the time, while he was patiently giving them lessons and noting their progress, he secretly planned another tour. Austria and its imperial court were already conquered, but there were other lands and other emperors and kings and dukes and lords. Austria was not the only musical country in Europe. Germany, France, England, Holland, and Italy were also great musical centers. It was to these lands that Papa Mozart planned to bring his "wonder children." In this way, he was certain fame and fortune would come to the Mozart family.

Leopold Mozart considered the tour to Vienna only a trial venture. He now knew how to travel, how to arrange for coaches and inns, how to get letters of introduction, how to prepare announcements for the press, and how to court favor. In those days everything depended upon the favor of royal patrons.

So it was that after a half-year of good solid practicing, the Mozart family again left Salzburg. It was

June of the year 1763 when the "grand tour" began, a tour which was to last over three years.

Shortly after starting out, when they were near Munich, the coach broke down and the Mozarts had to wait a whole day for it to be repaired. While they waited, Leopold took little Mozart to a church where, for the first time, the child saw an organ with a pedal keyboard. His father explained how the foot pedals sounded the low bass notes and how they worked, and Wolfgang was of course anxious to try this organ. He was so small that when he sat on the bench his feet could not reach the pedals. But he was determined. So he pushed the bench back and stood on the pedals, then, hopping quickly from one to another, he played and improvised many tunes. He was thrilled to hear the great bass notes that resounded with a thunderous roar through the stone nave of the church.

After that, Wolfgang asked permission to play on the local church organ in each town they passed through. When the Mozarts came to the old university town of Heidelberg they found a large crowd waiting at the church to hear the boy play. The news of this "wonder child" had traveled before them.

The dean and church canons invited little Wolfgang to give the people a concert on the organ. He played for a full hour and everyone was profoundly moved. Some said that such talent could only come from God, and the dean of the church ordered that the name of Wolfgang Mozart be inscribed on the organ to mark this occasion "as an eternal remembrance."

In another city through which they passed Leopold bought a new clavier on which his children could practice while they were traveling. It is difficult for us to find out exactly what kind of keyboard instrument the Mozarts used at different periods of Wolfgang's childhood. The family employed the word "clavier" loosely, and must have often meant the clavichord and even the harpsichord. In a clavichord, musical sounds result when small hammers, operated by the keys, are made to strike the strings. In a harpsichord, on the other hand, the strings are plucked by quills as the musician presses the keys.

By the time he was twenty-one, Mozart had expressed his enthusiasm for the pianoforte, forerunner of our modern piano, although he probably did not have access to this instrument while he was a child. In later life, however, he often used the word "clavier" when referring to any keyboard instrument. This may have been because he had become accustomed to the word during his childhood.

When the Mozart family reached the city of Frankfort, Leopold decided that here was a good place to display his "wonder children." He planned three concerts. Papa Mozart was a good press agent and he knew how to advertise his boy and girl so that they would attract an audience.

He wrote the following announcement which was published in the newspaper:

"The great admiration awakened in all audiences by the astounding genius of the two children of Herr Leopold Mozart has necessitated three concerts instead of the one previously announced. . . . The little girl, who is in her twelfth year, will play the most difficult compositions of the greatest masters. The boy, who is not yet seven, will perform on the clavier or harpsichord. He will also play a violin concerto and will accompany symphonies on the clavier, the manual or keyboard being covered with a cloth, with as much facility as if he could see the keys. Also, he will name exactly all notes played at a distance, singly or in chords, on the clavier or any other instrument, glass, bell, or clock. And finally, he will improvise on the harpsichord or organ in the most difficult keys as requested by the audience and for as long as desired. Tickets may be had at the Golden Lion. The price of admission is three marks."

It was this press notice that filled the hall. It was almost like a circus advertisement for acrobats and performing animals. In one small point only did Papa

Mozart make a false claim. His son was not under seven, but well into his eighth year.

The famous author, Goethe, then a youth, attended one of these concerts and many years later he recalled: "I saw Mozart as a seven year old boy when he gave a concert. . . . I was then about fourteen years old but I remember distinctly the little fellow with his powdered wig and his sword." From this we know that little Wolfgang was wearing the princely costume presented to him by the Empress Maria Theresa.

When the Frankfort concerts were over, the Mozarts traveled on through Germany, playing in one city after another. Princess Amalie, a sister of Frederick the Great, suggested that Leopold Mozart take his "wonder children" to Berlin. But Leopold thought that the German nobility were quite ignorant and very stingy. He wrote to a friend: "If the kisses that Princess Amalie bestowed on my children, especially on little Wolfgang, were gold pieces all would be well. But hotel bills and coaches cannot be paid with kisses." And so he decided not to take his children to Berlin. Instead they went to Brussels, where they stayed for three weeks.

Here again, Leopold was disappointed. He wrote to friends: "In Brussels it looks as though all were in vain, for His Royal Highness Prince Karl has promised to hear my children, but so far has not done so. He does nothing but hunt, eat, and drink, and so we may in the end discover that he has no money. I confess we have received many valuable presents here. We have so many snuff-boxes, leather cases, and other novelties that we could soon open a store."

Finding Brussels unprofitable, Leopold decided to waste no more time, but to go straight to Paris. The Mozarts arrived there on November 18, 1763.

The wife of the Bavarian Ambassador to France had originally come from Salzburg. She knew the Mozarts and invited them to stay at the Embassy. She also promised to introduce them to the court at Versailles.

In this year, 1763, Louis XV was on the throne of France. And in this year, also, the Seven Years' War came to an end—the war in which France lost most of her possessions in India and Canada to England. The people were happy that the fighting had at last ended. They were ready to enjoy the pleasures of life. Paris was friendly and gay. Music was in the air. It was the perfect moment for the Mozarts to arrive.

To avoid the deep mud and filth of the Paris streets, Papa Mozart hired three sedan chairs which were carried by strong men. In this regal manner he had himself and his two children carried about Paris to present his letters of introduction. But his efforts did not bring immediate results.

He was annoyed to see how slowly things moved in France. "Snail's post," he called it. However, after a month in Paris, his wish came true. On Christmas Eve the Mozarts were invited by the King to stay for two weeks at the famous palace of Versailles.

The little family from provincial Salzburg moved into the palace of the kings of France. They were dazzled by its rich splendor. The children thought it a fairyland. They saw the famous gardens with the fountains, the broad marble stairways, the long halls lined with rare tapestries and hundreds of brilliant mirrors, the sparkling chandeliers, and furniture carved and covered with pure gold leaf. And they saw the ladies and gentlemen of France dressed in silks, laces, and brocade and wearing priceless gems.

The Mozarts were awed by the splendor of Versailles. But they were surprised to find that in spite of the setting, the etiquette of the French court was quite informal. In Austria and in Germany they had become accustomed to bowing and bending the knee to show respect for the lord or sovereign. Here in France things were different. It was considered bad taste to bow and humble oneself before the King or Queen. This was the tradition of France. The Mozarts learned these new French manners quickly.

The Mozart children played for the King in his private apartments, and they also played for the Queen in her private apartments. The Queen's three daughters and the little Dauphin were often with her.

The Dauphin, who was later to become the unfortunate Louis XVI, was at this time only ten years old.

On other days Wolfgang and Nannerl played for the famous Madame Pompadour, one of the great ladies of the court. She too had her private apartments in the palace. The Mozarts were kept quite busy going from one apartment to another in the great palace of Versailles.

On New Year's Day the Mozarts were invited to attend the royal dinner. They were not invited to eat at the table, but were permitted to stand with the footmen and butlers behind the chairs of the King and Queen. This was considered a privilege and an honor.

During the dinner the Queen, who was Polish by birth, spoke to little Mozart in German and fed him one or two morsels from the lavish table as one might feed a puppy. The hall was freezing cold and the royal family and their titled guests were all dressed in furs. The men wore their large plumed hats at the table. But they were very polite and always tipped their hats before speaking to a lady.

At length the Mozarts' two weeks' visit at Versailles was over and they returned to Paris. Papa Mozart was very pleased. His children had won the hearts of all. And they had not been rewarded with snuff-boxes and other trifles. They had been presented with one thousand and two hundred silver livres! While this sum would amount to only two hundred and fifty dollars in our present money, in the days of Louis XV its purchasing value was many times greater.

Papa Mozart liked the King and Queen of France. He had found them friendly and generous. A week or two later he found that the French people were also generous. His "wonder children" gave concerts which brought in large profits, the equivalent of a thousand dollars in our money. Paris was a good place. Here his children were really appreciated.

Leopold Mozart, however, was not satisfied to rest on this success. He planned something more. He sent the manuscript pages of four of Wolfgang's sonatas to a music engraver.

"Imagine the sensation," he wrote to his friends in Salzburg, "these sonatas will make in the world when one reads on the title page that they were composed by a seven year old child. . . ."

In the expectation of favors to come, these first published works of Mozart were dedicated to two ladies of the highest French nobility. Papa Mozart knew only too well that all the arts depended upon patronage for survival. Without patronage they withered and died.

But while these practical things filled Papa Mozart's mind, little Wolfgang had other thoughts. In Paris he had heard French music and had attended the French opera. For him, this was new and different. It stirred his imagination. It filled him with ideas.

He too would write new music, music such as none had ever heard before!

After five full and profitable months in France, Papa Mozart decided to leave Paris and try his family's fortune in London. And so in April of the year 1764 the Mozarts traveled to the French coast and saw the ocean for the first time.

Very soon they were in a small sailing vessel bobbing up and down on the rough choppy channel. After many long and unpleasant hours they at last came into the quiet waters of a harbor and their vessel touched the shore of England.

The headstrong George III was on the English throne at this time. The Boston Tea Party did not take place until nine years later, but already this King was insisting on the heavy and unjust taxation of the thirteen American Colonies. But all this was politics and George III did not allow politics to interfere with his pleasures. He liked good food, hunting, and music.

Papa Mozart knew this. He also knew that Charlotte, the English Queen, who was a German girl, played the piano and sang quite well and that the King was a great admirer of Handel's music. It was, in fact, well known in musical circles that the composer Handel had left his native Germany to settle in England, where he had won the patronage of the royal family, serving first George I and later George

II. In time he was naturalized, becoming a British subject. All his finest music, including his *Water Music*, his *Royal Fireworks Music*, and his *Messiah* were written in England. He enjoyed the patronage of the kings of England and when he died he was buried in Westminster Abbey.

When the Mozarts reached London, Handel had been dead five years, but his music was very much alive. It was highly regarded by the public and was often performed. Everywhere the Mozarts went they heard Handel's music. Its fine inventive quality made a lasting impression on little Wolfgang, one which he never forgot. Handel's solid musical workmanship was also a good early influence. It showed Wolfgang how his own musical ideas could be worked out.

Two young German musicians then living in London became good friends of the child Mozart and also helped influence his musical education. Carl Frederick Abel had been a pupil of the famous Johann Sebastian Bach in Leipzig. He played the gamba and composed in the Bach manner. Wolfgang's second friend was Bach's youngest son, Johann Christian, an accomplished musician who wrote a good deal of church music, but not in the manner of his famous father. In fact his style has a strong Italian influence. It is not so ponderous as the German, and being lighter, freer, and sunnier, it pleased little Mozart.

All in all, the music Wolfgang heard in London

made a deep impression upon him. One can safely say that had this visit not taken place during Mozart's childhood, his music would have developed in other directions.

The Mozarts' London visit was fortunate in other ways. Wolfgang and Nannerl played at the court by royal command and they also gave some very successful public concerts.

King George and Queen Charlotte received them at St. James's Palace in a most friendly way and without formality. They brushed ceremony aside. The children and their parents were pleased at Their Majesties' warm-hearted manner.

After the first concert, the King ordered that Wolfgang and Nannerl be presented with twenty-four guineas (one hundred and twenty-five dollars), which Leopold Mozart considered a generous sum for a few hours of music. Soon after this first appearance, as they were all walking in the park, they were further honored. The King drove by in his carriage and, recognizing the Mozarts, nodded to them and with a smile greeted young Wolfgang.

In their second appearance at court the King put some of Handel's music before young Mozart. The child had never seen this music before, yet he played it perfectly at sight, astonishing the King and all who were present. After this, Wolfgang ran to the organ and played several other compositions with great mastery. This surprised the King still more. In the evening the child played again and he also accompanied the Queen in a song. Then, just to show his ability, he took a Handel bass part and improvised on it a beautiful melody. Now those present were more than astonished. They were amazed.

Having pleased King George and the court with his "wonder children," Papa Mozart now turned to the general public. Being a good showman, with a talent for advertising, he engaged a hall for the fifth of June, the day after the King's birthday. He knew that all society would be in London at this time and he lured this public with the following advertisement:

"For the benefit of Miss Mozart of Eleven and Master Mozart of Seven years of age, Prodigies of Nature. This method is therefore taken to show to the public the greatest Prodigy that Europe or that even Human Nature can boast of. Everybody will be struck with Admiration to hear them, and particularly to hear a Young boy of Seven Years of Age play on the Harpsichord with such Dexterity and Perfection. It surpasses all Understanding and all Imagination. . . . His father brought him to England not doubting but that he must meet with success in a Kingdom where his countryman Handel received during his life-time such particular Protection. Tickets at Half a Guinea each, to be had of Mr. Mozart at Mr. Cousin's Hair-cutter, in Cecil Court, St. Martin's Lane."

This announcement, printed in a London newspaper, attracted attention and also drew a crowd. People seemed ready to pay the half-guinea (two-and-a-half dollars), a high price for admission in those days, to see and hear this wonder of "Human Nature." They came, they heard, and they left satisfied. Leopold Mozart was pleased with his children's success and was able to send some of the profits of this concert back to Salzburg for safekeeping and to pay off a few of his debts. In gratitude to the English people for their generous support he allowed Wolfgang to take part in a charity concert for the benefit of a London hospital.

This time the advertisement read:

". . . he has already given Pleasure, Delight and Surprise to the highest Judges of Music in England, and is justly esteemed the most extraordinary Prodigy, and most amazing Genius that has appeared in any Age."

But this "amazing Genius" was still a child and often behaved like a child. One day as he was performing for some of the English nobility, he noticed a cat walking into the room. He stopped playing, ran from the keyboard, and picked up the cat. It was some time before he could be persuaded to return to his music.

Since leaving his home in Salzburg and living in Germany, France, and England, Wolfgang had heard a number of orchestras and he thought he would like to write a symphony of his own. He was only eight years old, but he had already acquired a sense of orchestration. But he had to perform almost every day and did not have the time to write out the music which was running through his mind.

One day, however, his ambitious and driving father went to bed with a heavy cold and Wolfgang finally had time to sit down and write his first symphony. As he was doing this he said to his sister Nannerl, who was sitting close by: "Be sure to remind me to give the horns plenty to do." He was a little afraid of horns. He found their sound overpowering and when he was very small he had often been frightened by their penetrating blasts. Now that he was eight, he knew that horns gave color and special accent to an orchestral work. In this, his first symphony, he wanted to show that he knew how the horns should behave.

During the weeks of his father's illness young Mozart worked secretly on this symphony, in which he was determined to keep the horns busy. When his father was better and out of bed, Wolfgang presented him with the manuscript of his Symphony No. 1 in E Flat Major!

During the summer months that followed, the boy managed to complete two more symphonies. These were not large works, nor were they important, but they showed that the young composer, only eight years old, had mastered the form, although he still had little to say that was different and original.

Some time later the Mozart children were again invited to play at the Court of St. James. They were asked to perform at an anniversary celebration of King George's accession to the throne. It was now four years since his coronation. In gratitude for the royal favor which his "wonder children" received, Papa Mozart had little Wolfgang's six violin sonatas printed and dedicated to Queen Charlotte from "her very humble and very obedient little servant."

Shortly after these successes, something happened in London which was to make a lasting impression upon Wolfgang and influence his entire future. This was the performances of the famous Italian opera.

Here was something new, something entirely different. The child had seen several operas in Paris and had loved them. But what he saw in the Italian opera in London captivated him completely. These operas were not serious like those he had seen before. They had humor, brilliance, and color.

Night after night the father and son, who had

walked up the marble steps of Versailles, and visited the Court of St. James, climbed the rough steep steps to the gallery of the Italian opera. Night after night they sat spellbound as they listened to the music and the singing of the great stars.

Here was a new form of composition to occupy Wolfgang's attention. He studied it carefully, and very soon, with his usual perception and genius, he felt that he knew and understood exactly how an opera should be written. In fact his creative mind already began planning an opera of his own. What the Italian composers could do he felt he could also do.

Soon it was time to leave London. The novelty of the Mozart "wonder children" was beginning to wear off, so Papa Mozart announced a "last and final" concert at reduced prices.

But before the Mozarts left London, the British Museum honored little Wolfgang by asking for a manuscript for their permanent collection and a picture of the child as a memento of his visit.

London was friendly. It was large, sprawling, and dirty, but it had received the Mozarts with open arms. Their visit had been a great success. In addition, the visit had made a lasting impression on Mozart and proved a turning point in his musical career. His impressionable mind was now overflowing with ideas.

In London he had met Bach's son and Bach's pupil,

Carl Frederick Abel, and had been inspired by their compositions. Here he had also heard the music of Handel, and the exciting Italian opera with its famous singers. Here he had found musical inspiration and a freedom from the conventional German forms. And here too in London he was inspired to write his first symphonies and plan his first opera.

London had been more than kind. It had proved a maturing influence on Mozart's musical development. When the Mozart family crossed the channel to return to the mainland of Europe little Wolfgang was a very different boy from the one who had left the sleepy town of Salzburg only a few years before.

He had been an honored guest at Versailles and at the Court of St. James. He had seen three great countries, Germany, France, and England, and had absorbed as much as he could of their cultures and their music.

He had found the big musical world. It was to this world that he felt he now belonged.

Before leaving England, Papa Mozart had accepted an invitation, through the Dutch Ambassador in London, to visit Holland. But the visit to this land was not very inspiring. Holland was musically under the influence of Paris and so did not contribute anything in particular to Mozart's development. His sojourn there did, however, indirectly give little Wolfgang time to compose.

The early winter climate of Holland was harsh, and both children became very ill, first Nannerl and then Wolfgang. When Wolfgang was recovering he asked for pen and paper, and while he was still in bed he recorded many of the musical ideas that were rushing through his fevered brain. He did not have to sit at a keyboard to write his music. Nor did he have to play it over to hear how it sounded. He could hear it in his mind as he was writing it.

In the short time that the Mozarts spent in Holland Wolfgang composed six sonatas for violin and piano. When he was fully recovered he gave a concert, the first concert in which he played only music which he himself had composed.

It was also during this visit that Leopold Mozart succeeded in having published a Dutch translation of his *Violin Method*.

And so, all in all, the visit to Holland, though marred by the severe illness of the two "wonder children," turned out to be fairly successful. It could not of course be compared to their visits to France and England, where they had won such glories, but it was better than being in Salzburg. Papa Mozart did not look forward to returning to this sleepy, provincial town after life in the big glamorous world outside. But they had been away for three years and his leave of absence was long over.

During these years the children had grown and developed musically. Never a day passed that they did not practice. Papa Mozart kept them working hard even when they were traveling. The little clavier was always the first piece of baggage brought down from the top of their coach.

To friends back in Salzburg, Leopold Mozart wrote: "You know my children are accustomed to work. Should they become idle then my whole edifice would fall apart."

He was proud of his "wonder children," but worried about returning home where their great talents could not be properly displayed and might not be appreciated. "Perhaps we shall be welcomed in such a way that we will gladly pack up and set off again. At any rate I am bringing my children back to their homeland. And if they are not wanted I am not to blame. It will be our country's loss."

So it was that after an absence of three years the Mozarts turned homeward. Little Wolfgang had been seven when they left and now he was almost eleven.

While he was already accomplished both as a performer and composer, in other ways he was still a child. Day after day, traveling across Europe in a coach, he looked out of the window and spoke to his sister. He imagined that all the rolling landscape was part of a beautiful fairyland where he was king and all the children of the land were his subjects. He had a clear idea of the shape of this fairyland, described it to his sister in detail, and invented very funny names for all the cities and different places.

But these imaginings were not the only thoughts which occupied Wolfgang on this homeward journey. As they rolled along he silently recalled many scenes of the "grand tour" now coming to an end. He saw again the streets of Paris and London, the homes of nobility, the sparkling fountains and glittering palace of Versailles, and the friendly Court of St. James. He heard again the applause and approval of the crowds that came to hear him play. And out of the rumble of the coach wheels and the rhythm of the horses' hoofs snatches of melody came back to his mind. He heard musical fragments from Handel, from the works of his two friends Carl Frederick Abel and Johann Christian Bach, and from the wonderful Italian operas. All this was new music, in a new style. And this he was now bringing home in his heart.

His father had taken him on a "grand tour" to display him. He was returning richly laden with musical inspiration.

1767   1769

Salzburg and Vienna

L eopold Mozart feared that, after being away
for three years, he might not find his job
waiting for him. Three years was a long leave
of absence.

But the Archbishop of Salzburg was kind, understanding, and generous. He listened to the adventures
of the Mozarts. He was very proud that little Wolfgang and Nannerl, natives of Salzburg and his own
subjects, should have acquitted themselves so honor-
ably before the ruling monarchs of France and England. Surely when these great monarchs heard little
Mozart play they must have thought of the Archbishop of Salzburg!

The Archbishop listened to the long adventures of
the grand tour and he examined the programs and
many of the press comments. But there was one thing

he found difficult to believe. He was sure the proud
father was exaggerating. He could not believe that
little Wolfgang could have distinguished himself as a
composer.

"It is the truth," insisted Papa Mozart. "Here are
his compositions. These he composed in France and
these in England. The six sonatas for violin and piano
he wrote in Holland."

"But surely you must have helped him?"

"Not at all."

"I know music, and it is not possible that these
scores were composed by a mere boy. Not possible!"

Then the Archbishop said that he would believe it
only if he saw it accomplished under his own eyes.
He proposed that Wolfgang be shut up in his palace
for a week with pen, ink, and music paper. He was to
see no one except the palace servants, who would
bring him his food and whatever else he might need.
During this week he was to produce a musical work.

"Very well. It is agreed," said Papa Mozart.
"What kind of composition would you like him to
write?"

"Let him write a sacred oratorio. I will myself
provide the words."

And so it happened that little Mozart was brought
to the Archbishop's palace. His room had in it a
clavier, a bed, a desk with a pile of music paper, and
pen and ink. He set to work. In seven days he was to
have finished an original composition, but he did not

need so much time. Before the week was over the boy had completed a score which filled two hundred and eight long sheets of music paper!

The Archbishop was amazed. Now he believed. He ordered that the oratorio should be copied out in its various parts and rehearsed by his court musicians. This was done, and a public performance was given during Lent.

The Archbishop was in the audience and he led the applause. It was his doubt that had given birth to a fine sacred composition. He himself had written the words, and his little subject had written the music. He was very proud.

Mozart's education was directed entirely by his father. He was never sent to school, nor did he have any tutors. Besides his lessons in music his father taught him to read and write. He also taught him simple arithmetic.

Through reading, Mozart acquired a taste for literature. He loved fantastic tales. When he was still quite young someone presented him with a copy of *The Arabian Nights*, and he read these tales of imagination with great delight. He also showed a talent for languages and, besides his native German, he soon was able to read and speak Latin, French, and Italian. He had a love for the dramatic. But of course his main love and interest was music. He learned no history, no geography. Neither did he learn any of the other subjects which children study in schools. He did not play games with other children, but spent his time at home. He found great delight in his music and did not have to be urged to practice. And he was never so happy as when he was composing. Rapidly and with little effort his pen filled sheets and sheets of music paper with notes and other musical notations.

During this creative process his imagination had full flight. The world which he created was rich with color, joy, and heavenly fleeting melody. At such times he soared above this world like a sun god.

Neither Papa Mozart nor Wolfgang was very happy in Salzburg.

For the father, work in the Archbishop's orchestra was tedious compared to life in Europe's gay capitals. Salzburg was a narrow place. He did not like the little jealousies among his fellow musicians; it was all so mean and petty. He dreamed of better things—more concerts and successes for his son. He dreamed that somewhere in the great world beyond Salzburg he would find a rich patron for Wolfgang. How else could an artist live!

And so Papa Mozart concentrated on his son's musical education. He felt that little Wolfgang needed more training in harmony and counterpoint. To accomplish this, he provided his son with a blank exercise book of ruled music paper. In this book he wrote out musical problems which the boy had to solve. Every week he made the problems more difficult. We can see how Wolfgang solved these problems and progressed, for this exercise book is preserved in the Mozart Museum.

For Wolfgang the long hours at home working out musical problems seemed dull and monotonous compared to that sparkling life he had tasted abroad. In Salzburg there were no great concert virtuosos such as he had met in Paris and London. There were no great singers and no Italian opera. Although he was still a child he longed for these things.

And so father and son joined in their dreams, and in the fall of the year 1767 they started out on a further adventure. Papa Mozart had succeeded in obtaining another leave of absence from the Archbishop and he hired a coach to take the whole family to Vienna, where a royal wedding was about to take place. He felt that since all the aristocracy of Europe would be present it would be a good time and place to display his son's talents.

The practice clavier was again tied to the top of a coach, together with trunks and boxes, and once more the family went traveling. Papa Mozart was hopeful, ever hopeful that fame and fortune was just over the hill.

Fame and fortune, however, were not waiting in Vienna. Shortly after the Mozarts arrived, and while

arrangements were being made for a brilliant series of
concerts, an epidemic of smallpox broke out, killing
hundreds of people. The young princess, who was
about to be married, died. And the court went into
deep mourning.

Papa Mozart fled with his family to Olmütz, a city
about a hundred miles north of Vienna. Thus he
hoped to escape the epidemic. But alas, it was not possible. Both the Mozart children had already con-
tracted the disease.

The children might easily have died had the Mozarts not found a true friend in Olmütz. The Dean of
the Cathedral of Olmütz, Count Podstatsky, at great
risk to himself and his family, took the Mozarts into
his home and sent for the best doctors to treat the
stricken children.

Both brother and sister were desperately ill. For
nine days Wolfgang was blind. But gradually both he
and Nannerl recovered. As soon as they were completely well, their father took them back to Vienna.
He had learned that the epidemic was over and he was
determined to carry through his plans for the concerts.

Back once more in Vienna, the Mozarts were invited to give a concert at the royal palace. This
pleased Papa Mozart. Royal patronage was the only
road open to him. He was ready to perform with his
"wonder children" in the hope of receiving a present
of money, or if not money then at least a gold snuff-

box which could be sold for money. He was very much like a servant trying to please a rich man in order to get a good tip. But one must forgive him, for in those days music was supported by the nobility, and not by the public.

The royal concert was a pleasant affair, but there were always difficulties. Papa Mozart complained about the aristocrats and also about the public. He thought many of the European nobility ungenerous and even mean and stingy. As for the public, Papa Mozart wrote home to say that the people of Vienna had little understanding. "They are not capable of appreciating serious music but are attracted only to tricks, burlesques, and cheap melodies. They lack understanding and reserve their applause for the shallow and the worthless." He wrote in this strong language because he felt that his son was not appreciated as much as he deserved.

Papa Mozart was also disturbed by the jealousy of the musicians in Vienna who refused to attend Wolfgang's concerts so that they could say that they had never heard him play and therefore could not possibly know if he was a genius or not. "You see," he wrote, "that is why they avoid us, for is they saw and heard him, then they would have to admit the truth."

Papa Mozart now began to realize that the path to glory would not be an easy one. Besides the deep lack of public understanding and the rivalry of other musicians, he felt that he was confronted with another problem. Although Wolfgang had played in all the great courts of Europe, it was becoming clear to his father that the nobility were not to be relied upon for support. When it pleased their whim they were glad enough to listen to a concert. But how could he gain permanent royal patronage for his boy?

These thoughts began to worry Papa Mozart very seriously. And he was right, for these same problems plagued Mozart to the end of his days. His whole life was tormented by the constant effort which he was forced to make in an attempt to gain royal patronage, public understanding, and fair acknowledgment from his fellow musicians.

Papa Mozart was not, however, completely discouraged. He still had great hopes for the future. And so he devised a plan for surmounting his three greatest difficulties in one bold stroke. If the twelve-year-old Wolfgang could receive a commission to compose an opera, then royal patrons would be impressed, the public might be pleased, and the rival musicians would be forced to admit that here was a boy composer who could rival the masters.

This, he thought, was a brilliant plan and it was toward this end that he now worked without rest. He was friendly with those who had influence, he whispered in royal ears, he pulled strings, and at length the Emperor, who truly believed that this idea was his own, gave a command that young Mozart was to compose an opera in the Italian manner.

The Emperor further ordered, and this was exactly what Papa Mozart wished, that young Mozart should conduct the first performance from his seat at the clavier.

This the Emperor felt would be a novelty such as Vienna had never before seen. The boy Mozart would write the opera, the public would enjoy it, and he, the Emperor, who had made it all possible, would bask in its glory.

And so the twelve-year-old Mozart joined forces with a librettist, in those days called a "theatrical poet." A contract was signed with the manager of the Vienna Opera House providing for a fee of a hundred ducats to be paid to the young composer.

Wolfgang began work without delay. To write an opera in the Italian manner had been his heart's desire.

The story of the opera, entitled *The Pretended Simpleton*, was light and filled with those standard comic situations which pleased the audiences of that day. In a surprisingly short time the boy had completed all three acts of the musical score, containing twenty-five numbers and filling six hundred and fourteen sheets of music paper.

Even before the opera was finished there were ob-

jections. First of all, some of the musicians employed
by the Opera House, men without genius who spent
their lives sawing away on their fiddles, objected.
Their dignity was hurt. They did not think that a
twelve-year-old boy could write music good enough
for them. And the singers, many of whom were unable to read music and had to learn their songs by ear,
also objected. They said the arias were not suitable
and that they did not want the orchestra conducted
by a boy.

At the first rehearsal they all played and sang off-
key and in other ways tried to prove the music
worthless. The manager of the Opera House knew
that the music was good, but he was helpless against
so much opposition, and in the end he was forced to
put another opera in rehearsal in place of the one
written by Mozart.

This rejection was very hard for both father and
son. It was depressing. It had cost the family a good
deal of money to stay in Vienna, and now the hundred
ducats they expected to get for the opera would not
be paid.

To add to their troubles, Papa Mozart received
notice from Salzburg that his salary had been sus-
pended and would not be resumed until he returned
home. This made him very angry. In the heat of his
anger he sat down and wrote the Archbishop a sharp
letter. "His highness does not employ cheats, fakers
and liars in his service and then grant them his gra-

cious permission to visit foreign lands in order to throw dust into the public's eyes. No, those in his service are respectable men who travel only for the glory of their prince and country in order to show the world what a miracle God has performed in Salzburg in the creation of two wonder children."

But the Archbishop was not impressed by this letter. He was not going to pay any more salary to one who overstayed his leave of absence.

However, this visit to Vienna was not completely unsuccessful. Some good did come of it. It had become known throughout the country that the twelve-year-old boy had written an opera at the request of the Emperor. And because of this a distinguished Austrian physician, Dr. Mesmer, ordered Mozart to write him a little opera to be performed in the private theater he had had built in his gardens. Dr. Mesmer was very famous in Europe for his work in hypnotism, and the word "mesmerism" has now become part of our language.

Young Mozart began work at once on a one-act opera entitled *Bastien and Bastienne*. This did not turn out to be a very original or distinguished work, but it gave young Mozart a chance to show his talent as a composer of opera and marks his very first performance in this field.

Besides these two operas, the boy Mozart completed several other compositions before leaving Vienna. He wrote rapidly and with little effort. In a

short space of time he produced three symphonies
and a Solemn Mass which was performed at the
dedication of a new chapel in the orphan asylum.
This Mass he conducted himself in the presence of
the Emperor and many distinguished guests. But we
do not know today what this Mass sounded like, for
the music is lost. Perhaps some day it will be found.

With these successes still in the air, Papa Mozart
decided that it was a good time to leave Vienna. He
had originally planned to take his family to Italy,
at that time the musical center of all Europe. But now
he postponed the trip. He felt that he should hurry
back to Salzburg and make peace with the Archbishop. And so the Mozarts left Vienna and returned
to little Salzburg.

Papa Mozart had expected to find the Archbishop
quite angry because he had stayed away so long and
had written such a sharp letter. But the Archbishop
was a man of generous nature. He welcomed the Mozarts and in all ways showed that he was very proud
of the accomplishments of his Salzburg prodigy. He
even ordered that the opera, *The Pretended Simpleton*,
the very first that Mozart had written, should be performed by his own musicians in his palace.

Young Mozart conducted the orchestra and singers.
The performance was a great success, and the Archbishop was so pleased that he appointed young Mozart, a boy of thirteen, *Kapellmeister* of his orchestra,

though without pay. The *Kapellmeister* was from time to time called upon to compose special church music. He also rehearsed the choir and served as general assistant to the concertmaster who, in small orchestras, was the conductor.

In Salzburg the older musicians did not complain because the young boy was given a position of importance in their orchestra. They recognized and freely admitted Mozart's musical genius. There was no denying that as a performer, composer, and interpreter, regardless of his age, the boy was phenomenal.

"Only in Italy will he find his rivals," said Papa Mozart.

And so Papa Mozart began to dream again of another tour, more concerts, more conquests. This time he would take Wolfgang to the place where music had roots and a long tradition.

For two hundred years, Italy had been the wellspring of European musical ideas and forms. And in Italy music had become part of the national life and culture. Here were great schools for musical education, great theaters for operas, fine orchestras, and famous churches where music was a sacred tradition. To conquer musical Germany, France, and England had been comparatively easy. But to conquer Italy, that would be something different!

. . .

With this new dream of future glory the father and son began their daily routine for the Archbishop: rehearsals, teaching pupils, arranging old music, writing new music, and playing in the orchestra. They knew that they would have to work a long time before the Archbishop would consent to another leave of absence from his court. And so they toiled on, secretly planning and dreaming.

After about a year of hard work they finally felt that the time had come when they might safely ask the Archbishop for further leave. They confided to him their great desire to visit Italy and win new glories. And the Archbishop, who had a good heart, was pleased to grant their request.

This time, to save expenses, it was decided that Nannerl and her mother should remain at home. And in December of the year 1769 the father and son set out together to visit Italy, land of their dreams. In another month Wolfgang would be fourteen years old.

Young Mozart was very glad to be traveling once again. From the first post-station he wrote home to his mother: "My heart is filled with pure joy because our journey is a happy one and because it is warm in the coach and our coachman is a wonderful fellow who, when the road allows, lets out the horses and they run like the wind."

He was happy to be free of the confining atmosphere of the kind Archbishop's court. He was happy to be free of little Salzburg. He was happy to be going once more into the world he loved, a world which was wide and stimulating and where he could meet fellow artists of his own stature. He was happy to be going to Italy, the land of music.

1769   1771

The Italian Tour

Italy welcomed both father and son. Their tour of
the Italian peninsula, which lasted a little over a
year, was to prove one of the happiest periods in
Mozart's life. Everything about it was good.

At Verona he played in the finest homes. A local
nobleman was so impressed with the boy that he
ordered an artist to paint his portrait. Mozart also
played on the two organs in the old church of San
Tomaso. Such a great crowd had gathered to hear
him that he and his father could hardly get out of the
coach.

At Mantua Mozart played in the Philharmonic Society's concert hall. It was here that, for the first
time, he heard several of the great women concert
singers of Italy. He accompanied them at the clavier

in such a way as to best display their voices, and they were very pleased. When he was leaving Mantua one of the singers wept and another sent him a small jar of pomade for his chapped hands together with a little poem. They wanted to show their appreciation and genuine affection.

Wolfgang then gave successful concerts in Milan, Bologna, and Florence. As a result of all this, he was given a commission to write an opera for the Milan Opera House. The libretto was on the subject of "Mithridates, King of Pontus." The work was to be ready by the end of the year and he was to receive one hundred ducats and free lodgings during the rehearsals and production. This time he felt confident that his work would be appreciated. He would not be forced to face the humiliation he had suffered in Vienna. While at Bologna, he studied fugue with the great teacher and scholar, Padre Martini.

And so it was with light hearts that father and son worked their way down the Italian boot and arrived in Rome in time for Holy Week.

On Wednesday and Thursday they went to the Sistine Chapel at St. Peter's to hear the famous *Miserere* which had been written over a century before by the Italian composer Allegri.

So sacred was this composition that the Vatican singers and musicians were forbidden to carry home any part of the music on pain of excommunication.

But young Mozart did not feel that this regulation applied to him. He sat in the Sistine Chapel under the famous Michelangelo ceiling and listened intently to the music. Not a single note escaped him. Then, hurrying back to the hotel, he took up pen and paper.

"What are you going to write?" asked his father.

"The *Miserere*."

"Can you remember it?"

"The notes of every part are clear in my head. I can write it all out from memory."

After Wolfgang had written out the *Miserere*, he was eager to check its correctness. He and his father returned to the Sistine Chapel on Good Friday and with the score secreted in his hat, young Mozart followed the music. The notes he had written from memory were almost perfect. Only one or two minor corrections were needed.

The report that young Mozart had written down the music of the sacred *Miserere* quickly spread through Rome, and he was asked by the Vatican to produce his copy. It was found to be correct in every detail. Soon all Rome knew of this amazing feat.

When this news reached Salzburg, Mozart's mother and sister were filled with horror. They believed that he had sinned and would be excommunicated. However, Papa Mozart hastened to calm their fears. "We both had a good laugh when we read your letter," he wrote. "There is nothing to worry about. It is taken in quite another way. All Rome knows about it. Even the Pope himself. . . . There is certainly nothing to be afraid of for it has brought him great honor. . . . Be sure to show this letter everywhere in Salzburg so that the true facts are known."

Wolfgang was in high spirits. He wrote long letters home filled with little drawings, nonsense rhymes, and words that he invented only because he liked their sound. His heart was happy. He sprinkled his letters with Italian and Latin words and sometimes invented the craziest and most absurd expressions.

After visiting St. Peter's he wrote to his sister: "I have had the honor of kissing the foot of the statue of St. Peter, but since I have the misfortune to be so short, your good old Wolfgang Mozart had to be lifted up!"

From Rome Papa Mozart and his son traveled to Naples, where Wolfgang continued to give concerts and impress the public with his incredible talent. On one occasion an old woman in the audience called out: "It is all magic! And the magic is due to the ring on his finger."

To prove that she was wrong Wolfgang took off his ring and showed that he could play just as well without it. The audience broke into loud applause.

But his life in Italy was not all admiration and applause. After leaving the glamorous concert halls he and his father had to return to their simple little lodgings.

From Naples he wrote his sister:

"Vesuvius is smoking fiercely! Thunder and lightning and blazes! . . . Now I will describe to you how we live. I rise generally every morning at 9 o'clock, but sometimes not until 10, at which time we go out. We eat in a restaurant. After dinner I write, and I write until it is time for supper. And what do we eat? Half a fowl or a slice of roast meat. On fast days a little fish. After supper we go to sleep. Now you understand how we live. . . . In the opera house we often see the King of Naples. He is short and because of this he always stands on a stool so that he may look a little taller than the Queen. The Queen is beautiful and most gracious for she bowed to me a number of times."

After many successful concerts and pleasant adventures in Naples the father and son returned to Rome. This journey was usually made in slow stages and took over four days, but Wolfgang and his father took the fast coach and made the trip in only twenty-seven hours. And since they were able to get only two hours of sleep and very little food, they arrived exhausted and hungry.

The next morning as soon as it was known that the

young Mozart had returned to Rome, a courier arrived from the Vatican inviting father and son to have an audience with the Pope. During this visit the Pope conferred on Wolfgang the Order of the Golden Spur. This order brought with it a gold medal and the title *Signor Cavaliere*. It was a very high honor and Wolfgang was very proud. Some years earlier the composer Gluck had also received this distinction, but he was forty-two years old when he was made a *Signor Cavaliere*. No musician fourteen years of age had ever before been so honored by the Vatican.

When Papa Mozart and his son returned to their lodgings they were in very high spirits. Mozart wrote a brief note to his sister just so that he could sign it with the following words: "I have the honor to be your very humble servant and brother the Cavaliere Mozart."

All this was good fun. Papa Mozart often smiled when he heard people addressing his young son as *Signor Cavaliere.* He smiled because Wolfgang seemed such a little Cavaliere, but nevertheless he was very proud of the title and insisted that his son use it whenever he signed his name.

But young Mozart was very modest and felt that titles added little or nothing to a person's true artistic worth. He used the title merely to be obedient and please his father. However, he soon forgot about it and after a year or two he left it off completely.

• • •

A few months after Mozart had been honored by the Vatican, he received another honor which he prized above all. His fellow composers, members of the Academy of Bologna, subjected him to a very severe examination in which he was locked in a room by himself and asked to compose a section of a Mass on a given theme. This difficult task he did very easily, completing the work in half-an-hour, although three full hours were allowed.

After the work was examined by a committee of composers, young Mozart was unanimously voted a member academician of the Bologna Philharmonic Society. This was the highest honor his fellow musicians could bestow upon him. Of this honor he was truly proud.

Young Mozart was completely happy in Italy. He wrote long letters to his mother and sister and filled them with bubbling nonsense. He sent complicated messages to the dog and to the pet canary. However he had one regret—his bad handwriting. "I can't write any better for this pen is not a writing pen but a music-note pen. I do not have any other."

But if Mozart's music pen was not good for writing letters it was very fine for writing music.

During the short time that he spent in Italy he composed four symphonies in the Italian manner and a number of arias and other compositions, besides the opera which had been commissioned for the Milan

Opera House. The great successes he had enjoyed in the past months and the appreciation he had received had encouraged him, and music flowed easily from his pen. Writing music was creation. And while creating he knew true happiness.

At length it was time to go to Milan to rehearse the singers and orchestra. And as is usual in every opera house, there were serious rivalries among the singers. Some thought they had not been given important roles to sing and others felt slighted because their arias were too short. The prima donnas were jealous of each other and the lesser singers all wanted to be prima donnas. Every day a new storm swept across the stage.

But young Mozart was very tactful. He was agreeable to everyone and tried to please all. For one singer he put in some extra high notes so that she could display herself and for another he wrote in a few sweet sentimental lines certain to bring applause. In this way all were eventually pacified, and everyone set to work to learn their words and music.

On the day after Christmas, in the year 1770, the opera *Mithridates, King of Pontus* was produced. Young Mozart conducted from the orchestra pit. The public was so pleased that many shouted as they applauded. They shouted "Bravo!" and "Long live the master!"

Here in Milan young Mozart had matched his musical talent with the best in Italy and had succeeded. Twenty performances were given.

Papa Mozart was very proud of his son. He felt that this success would establish Wolfgang firmly in the musical world. He believed the road would be easy from now on. With the reputation thus gained, commissions for musical compositions would come freely. The Italian critics had often said that it was impossible for a German to write an Italian opera. But here it was. The impossible had been accomplished. And with the impossible would come fame, glory, and money! The dream was now sure to come true.

Two good things did result from the success of this opera. The manager of the Milan Opera House commissioned the young composer to write another opera to be produced in the season of 1773. And Mozart also received a commission to write a dramatic serenade to be performed in honor of the coming marriage in Milan of the Archduke Ferdinand of Austria.

These honors mark the climax of Mozart's boyhood fame. He had spent his fourteenth and fifteenth birthdays in friendly Italy, and now he was no longer a boy. Gone were the days when he could be exhibited as a child prodigy by his proud and ambitious father! But with the great success of his opera and with many important compositions to his credit, he

7 1

felt ready to take his place as a man in the musical world. The glory of his childhood triumphs was now behind him. Fresh glories, he was sure, lay ahead.

And so—basking in the warmth of success—the happy travelers left Italy and returned to their home in Salzburg.

Five months later, on August 31, 1771, Mozart and his father again left Salzburg for Milan to compose the pastoral and mythological serenade which Wolfgang had been commissioned to write for the marriage of the Archduke Ferdinand.

The trip was a gay and pleasant one. Wolfgang visited with the celebrated opera composer, Hasse, who had also been commissioned to prepare an opera for the festivities. Hasse is said to have remarked, "This boy will cause us all to be forgotten."

The music for the serenade was light and gay. It was tuneful. The characters were gods and goddesses of ancient mythology. And it was well received by the public.

On the strength of this success, and knowing how unhappy Wolfgang was at the thought of returning to work for the Archbishop, Papa Mozart approached the Archduke and suggested that he take Wolfgang into his service and appoint him concertmaster of his orchestra.

But the Archduke could not make up his own mind. He asked the advice of his mother the Empress. And she, the Empress Maria Theresa, who had once dressed Nannerl and Wolfgang in brocades, she whom the child Mozart had kissed, now wrote, warning her son. She wrote that he should not hamper his court by giving positions to "useless people," people who would only dishonor his name by running about like beggars.

With this sharp advice from his mother, the Archduke Ferdinand refused to give Wolfgang a place in his orchestra. And so the father and son were forced to return to Salzburg and resume their duties in the Archbishop's court, arriving December 15, 1771.

1772   1777

Work, Bondage, and the Dream of Freedom

The day after Papa Mozart and his brilliant son returned to Salzburg, the good Archbishop died. He had been understanding and tolerant and proud of young Mozart. And now, much to everyone's surprise and disappointment, a very unpopular and mean dignitary was sent to fill his place.

The new Archbishop bore the imposing name and title of Hieronymous Joseph Franz von Paula, Count of Colloredo and Bishop of Gurk. This sounded very grand, but the man himself was stupid and petty. He had no conception of music or appreciation of Mozart's talent. And from the very first day the sensitive Mozart suffered under the pressure of this man's ignorance.

Nevertheless, Mozart performed his duties as *Kapellmeister* with full generosity. He did the very best he could, even composing an allegorical opera on a classical theme for the installation of the new Archbishop. Although he was taken seriously ill while he was working on this project he finished it in time: it consisted of ten arias, two choruses, and a full overture.

Mozart tried to please the new Archbishop, but it was impossible. He was not interested in music. He liked hunting, sports, and society. The brilliant young composer and musician working in his orchestra meant little or nothing to him. He did, however, recognize Mozart's ready pen and ordered him to keep busy writing new Masses and church music, as well as special pieces for the many holy occasions of the year. For this extra work Mozart should have received additional compensation, but the Archbishop extracted a full measure of services for the miserable wages of one hundred and fifty gulden a year which he paid him. This would amount to about two hundred and eighty dollars in our money. And although its purchasing value was greater in Mozart's day, it was barely enough, together with Papa Mozart's wages, to support the family. Servants were paid little less.

The tension was broken when Mozart and his father again left Salzburg in October 1772 for a third visit to Milan, to write the opera commissioned the preceding year. On this trip Leopold attempted to secure his son a post with the Grand Duke Leopold of Tuscany, but his efforts failed, and March 1773 they had to return to the Archbishop's oppressive court.

However, that summer young Mozart was again, for a short time, released from bondage. He and his father were given another leave of absence to go to Vienna. Wolfgang was now seventeen and his father was determined to make a final attempt to find him a patron. But again he failed.

Mozart was once more plunged into the routine work of the Archbishop's orchestra.

The past two years had been especially hard for Mozart because he had had to contend not only with the Archbishop but also with the jealousy of his fellow musicians at the court. When he was a "wonder child" they had accepted him and even been proud of him. But now they seemed to resent his presence. They looked upon him with envy because he had been received in the royal courts of Europe. They were quick to criticize, and they even poisoned the Archbishop's mind with false and malicious opinions. And the ignorant Archbishop in his crude and offensive manner set himself up as a critic and judge. "You know nothing about music," he said to Mozart one day. "You ought to go to a *conservatoire* in Italy and learn how to compose properly!"

In an atmosphere so highly charged with hostility

and insult, Mozart found it difficult to work. He was of a very sensitive nature, and his feelings were easily hurt. His creative spirit was being crushed. He began to dream of escape.

While this period of Mozart's life was very unhappy, yet it was one in which his music made some very important strides. Scholars have pointed out that it was during those days that the first signs of that quality which we call Mozartean began to appear in his work.

Before reaching the age of fifteen Mozart had written over one hundred compositions. But much of this early work was conventional and cast in the accepted musical forms of the day. It showed promise, though hardly that rare quality of creative imagination so characteristic of his later work. There was little display of musical originality. As one critic remarked: "The fruit was more extraordinary than excellent."

However, during the two years that followed his fifteenth birthday, his work suddenly matured. At this time he wrote a great quantity of music, some of which has become immortal. He wrote six piano sonatas for the newly improved pianoforte. All these have become very well known and are today part of every good piano library. During this time he also wrote seven symphonies.

It should be noted here that some of these orchestral works show the influence of Joseph Haydn, whose compositions Mozart greatly admired. Haydn was twenty-four years older than Mozart and was well established as a composer. It was natural that Mozart should at this formative time have been influenced by his work. But this influence was only a steppingstone to something more individual. His compositions soon lost all trace of Haydn's influence.

Haydn lived for eighteen years after Mozart died and it is interesting to see that his later music was definitely influenced by Mozart! In both cases the influence was a healthy one and marked musical progress.

As the months and years ran by, Mozart's dream of freedom grew stronger. He began to dislike everything in Salzburg, even the sight of its streets and its simple people.

The Archbishop must have sensed this, but he did not relent. In his deep ignorance he only became more and more critical and more and more demanding. At length Mozart could endure it no more and he wrote a long letter to the Archbishop resigning his position.

The Archbishop was furious. He knew that he could not replace young Mozart. And in anger he cried: "Both the son and the father can go seek their fortunes where they please!"

Papa Mozart was very upset. He feared that he would lose his position. He had no savings and desperately needed his small wages to support Mamma Mozart and Nannerl. It was a question of daily bread. But the Archbishop's anger soon cooled, and Leopold Mozart was permitted to keep his post in the orchestra.

Mozart, now free of his chains, began to make plans for the future.

He decided to go to Germany and Paris to seek his fortune. He was confident that somewhere abroad he would find an appreciative patron. After all, he was an accomplished artist. He was only twenty-one years old and he had already composed symphonies, operas, quartets, and concertos. He had written music for the piano, violin, horn, and other instruments. He had also written sacred music for the organ and church choirs. And he was justly proud of its quality; it could be compared with the best. Besides, he was a concert virtuoso. He could play the clavier and piano with grace and great technical skill. There was no one in Europe who could rival him in this!

Papa Mozart knew all this to be true, and he felt it was right for Wolfgang to leave Salzburg to seek his fortune elsewhere. Yet he did not like to be separated from his son and he feared to trust him alone in the big world. After all, Wolfgang had always led a sheltered life. The father had always been at his son's elbow, telling him what to do and what not to do. He had taken care of everything. How could the boy possibly manage alone!

And so Papa Mozart decided that Nannerl should stay in Salzburg to keep house for him, while Wolfgang, under his mother's protection, should journey forth to seek fortune from music's magic sounds.

On the twenty-third of September, 1777, Wolfgang and his mother left Salzburg. Mozart was happy to leave it behind. He was hopeful. He was certain that his talents would open many important doors.

Mozart was also happy to be traveling once more. He loved the rumble of the wheels, the sway of the coach, the sound of the horses' hoofs, and the moving landscape. These were things that he had originally heard and loved when he was six years old and had started out for the first time with Nannerl and his father. These were pleasant things which were part of his memories of the days when he and his sister were "wonder children."

The Last Grand Tour

rriving in Munich, Mozart sought an audience with the Elector of Bavaria, Maximilian Joseph. This was the same Maximilian Joseph for whom he and Nannerl had played when they were young. He hoped that this man might now become his patron. But all his efforts seemed in vain. He could not gain a private interview; the Elector was always too busy to see him. And he was finally forced to accept a humiliating compromise. Some friends arranged that he should wait in a small passageway through which his Royal Highness was to pass on his way to chapel. In this place he could perhaps have a few hurried words with the Elector.

Mozart waited nervously and impatiently. At length his Royal Highness appeared. He was irritated at being stopped. He and his gentlemen attendants were dressed in their hunting costumes and were eager to go on.

"Will your Royal Highness permit me to pay homage and lay myself and my services at your feet?" spoke Mozart, bowing low.

"You are Mozart," said the Elector, recognizing him. "So you have left Salzburg?"

"I have left it forever, your Royal Highness."

"Why? Have you had a row?"

"I asked permission to make this journey and it was refused. Therefore, I was compelled to take this step, although I have long intended to leave Salzburg."

"Good heavens, young man! But your father is still in Salzburg?"

"Yes, your Highness, and he humbly commends himself to you. I have already been in Italy three times and I have written three operas. I have the honor to be a member of the Academy of Bologna and was successful in my examination, having accomplished in a half-hour a composition which many have required three or four hours to produce. This alone would be sufficient proof of my ability to serve any court. My greatest wish is to be allowed to serve your Royal Highness."

"But my good young friend, I am sorry but at the

moment there is no vacancy. If only there were a vacancy!"

"I can assure your Royal Highness that I would do credit to Munich."

"Yes. No doubt. But there is no vacancy."

The Elector and his gentlemen in attendance, anxious to get on with the Mass and be free to go to the hunt, moved toward the door.

Mozart bowed respectfully. There was nothing more to be said.

Mozart was ready to serve a master, ready to pour out his genius. The Elector had refused him but he was confident that he would find some other patron in Munich. He was not disheartened.

He wrote to his father: "I have a great desire to write an opera again. . . . Composition remains my one and only passion and joy. I have only to go into the opera house and hear the orchestra tuning up and an uncontrollable desire comes over me." He was filled with music. Hundreds of original melodies floated through his mind.

Fearing that his son was perhaps not serious enough, Papa Mozart wrote to remind him that life was difficult and that money was very important. "Money-making must occupy your full attention. Otherwise a journey turns out to be of no profit and may even bring a man into debt."

But all such warnings were unnecessary. Mozart

knew that his father was already in debt, having sacrificed everything so that his son could make this journey. His father had provided him and his mother with good clothes and luggage, for he knew it was important to look successful when seeking favor. Mozart keenly felt the need of earning money, and went from place to place offering his services. But no one would have him.

The elder Mozart then imagined that there must be secret enemies, jealous musicians, working against his son in Munich. He therefore suggested that Wolfgang move to some other city where there might be less prejudice.

And so mother and son left Munich and went on to Mannheim, the seat of the German Prince Carl Theodor, whose orchestra was known to be the finest in all Europe.

Prince Carl Theodor was a man with genuine respect for art, music, literature, and science. He had been educated by the Jesuits and, in his early years, had been a friend of Voltaire. Besides lavishing great sums of money on his orchestra, he built a fine theater, engaged the best dramatists and actors, and established an opera house. The beautiful palace which he built for himself was called a "German Versailles."

It was said that this culture-loving Prince had spent over thirty-five million gulden on art and science, all of which had been raised by taxation. His subjects, who had to pay for it, did not share their Prince's love for culture. Nevertheless Mannheim was established as a center of music and drama, and it was to this place that Mozart now journeyed.

Against ignorance he felt helpless. But in a place like Mannheim, a seat of music and culture, he was sure he would find recognition.

The Mannheim orchestra was truly the best in all Europe. It was described by a music critic of the day as supreme. "Their *forte* is a thunder. Their *crescendo* a rushing waterfall. Their *diminuendo* a crystal stream babbling away into the far distance. Their *piano* the soft life giving breath of spring."

This orchestra has become famous in the history of music for having introduced a new style of playing. It gave accent to the dramatic and developed a long range of gradations between the very softest *pianissimo* and brutally crashing *fortissimos*. Such contrasts had not been known before. Here was a new musical conception built on emotional excitement. The Mannheim Orchestra was changing musical ideas. It was helping to liberate orchestral music from its narrow forms.

Prince Carl Theodor welcomed Mozart at his court and was delighted with his playing. Every time Mozart performed the Prince came close to the piano to watch his rapid fingers.

One day he said to Mozart: "I hear that in Munich you wrote an opera."

"Yes, your Highness, that is so. My greatest wish now is to write another opera. I beg your Highness not to forget me."

"Well, some day. . . ."

But while the Prince did not commission Mozart to write an opera, he did consult him about the musical education of his children. He even got Mozart to give them several lessons on the clavier. And Mozart was often invited to give performances at the court, where his playing charmed all.

But soon the dream of Mannheim began to fade. Mozart's brilliant performances and original music brought him nothing but a few presents.

"I wish I had received money instead," he wrote to his father. "One needs money traveling. I have received five watches! And I have a good mind to have an extra pocket made and wear two watches so that people will see that I do not need another."

When the father heard the sad news that his son had received only watches, he sent advice to go on to Paris and not tarry any longer in Mannheim. Months had been wasted and the hope of finding employment in this German center of musical culture now seemed shattered. Mozart had wished so ardently that the Prince would appoint him court composer. Members of the court had urged this appointment. But in the end nothing had come of it.

[ABOVE] *View of the town and citadel of Salzburg, 1795. Engraving by Anton Amon after a drawing by Franz Naumann.*

[LEFT] *Photograph of Mozart's birthplace.*

Anna Maria Mozart, the composer's mother. Un-signed portrait painted about 1775.

Leopold Mozart, the composer's father. Unsigned portrait painted about 1770.

Mozart at the age of six (1762) in a court dress given to him by the Empress Maria Theresa.

Mozart's sister, Nannerl, at the age of eleven (1762) in a court dress given to her by the Empress Maria Theresa.

Autograph manuscript of the Minuet in G (K.1), written in 1762.

Leopold, Wolfgang, and Nannerl at Paris, 1764. Engraving by Delafosse after a watercolor by Carmontelle.

Mozart at about the age of thirteen (ca. 1768). Portrait by Thadäus Helbling.

AMADEO WOLFGANGO MOZART ACCAD.FILARMON DI BOLO
VERONA

Mozart at the age of twenty-one (1777), wearing the Order of the Golden Spur. A copy that Mozart sent to his old teacher Padre Martini at Bologna, from a lost original painted at Salzburg.

The Mozart family at Salzburg in 1780. Hanging on the wall is a portrait of the composer's late mother. Print after a painting by J. N. della Croce.

*Constanze Mozart, née Weber, in 1783, the year of
her marriage. Lithograph after a lost miniature.*

Mozart, about 1783. Unfinished portrait by Joseph Lange, Mozart's brother-in-law.

Employers
of
Mozart

Hieronymous Colloredo, Prince-Archbishop of Salzburg

Joseph II, King of Germany and Holy Roman Emperor.

Theatrical Associates
of
Mozart

Emanuel Schikaneder, librettist and producer of The Magic Flute. *He played the part of Papageno in the original production.*

Lorenzo da Ponte, author of the librettos for The Marriage of Figaro, Don Giovanni, *and* Così fan tutte.

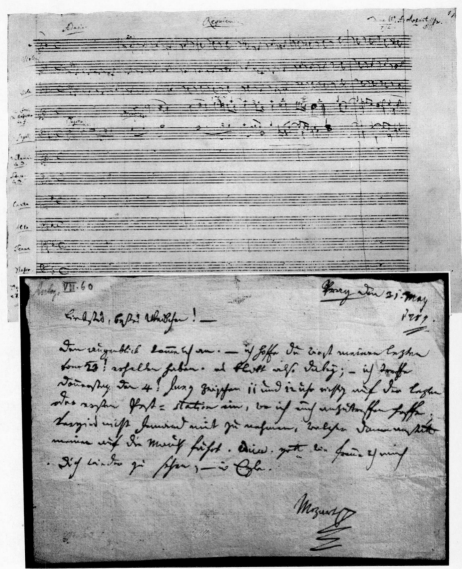

[ABOVE] *First page of the autograph score of the* Requiem (K.626), *Mozart's last composition, unfinished at his death.*

[BELOW] *Letter from Mozart to his wife, written in Prague, May 31, 1789.*

The last authentic portrait of Mozart. Drawing in silverpoint by Dorothy Stock, done at Dresden on April 17, 1789.

Mozart monument by Victor Tilgner at Vienna.

"Go to Paris," his father wrote, remembering the success his "wonder children" had had at the French court. "From Paris, the name and fame of a man of talent echoes throughout the world. In Paris the nobility treat men of genius with respect and honor. In Paris you encounter a life that contrasts greatly with the blunt coarse manners of our German gentlemen and their ladies."

There were still other advantages in going to Paris. Here Wolfgang could perfect himself in the French language and also find many eager amateurs who would be happy to have him give them lessons in both composition and playing. Then, too, Paris was a good market for the publication of musical compositions. But Papa Mozart felt that the French taste in music must be studied so that the public could be supplied with what was pleasing. "After all," he wrote, "even Voltaire reads his poems to his friends and listens to their criticism. And this too you must do if you want to make money."

Then, once more fearing that his son was too easygoing and perhaps not serious enough, he sent him a sharp warning. "Remember," he wrote, "the object of your journey is to assist your parents and contribute to your dear sister's welfare as well as to further your career and acquire honor and fame in the world, which you in some degree did in your boyhood. And now it rests entirely with you to raise yourself to one of the highest positions ever attained by any musician. . . . Therefore get off to Paris without delay. And take your place by the side of truly great people."

Young Mozart could tarry no longer. He engaged a coach to take his mother and himself to Paris by the shortest possible route. And after a wearisome journey of nine and a half days, on March 23rd, 1778, they arrived in Paris.

Paris

Now, thank Heaven! We are at our destination!" were the first words Mozart wrote from Paris to his father. "And now I trust, with the help of God, all will go well."

The Paris that Mozart had known fourteen years before, he now found greatly changed. There were many people in Paris who still remembered the "wonder child." But they were slow to accept him as a mature composer and concert virtuoso; they somehow could not believe that the great talents he had shown as a child could have survived. This was very annoying. And Mozart soon realized that it would take some time to dispel this attitude and reestablish himself.

To achieve this end, his friends introduced him to

members of the aristocracy with the object of having him play at their homes. In this way they hoped he could display his mature musical talents. These free private recitals they hoped would make his name and music better known in Paris.

At last, after much social maneuvering, it was arranged that he play for the important Duchess de Bourbon and her guests. But when he arrived, the room was cold as ice and there was no fire in the grate. "The windows and doors were open," he wrote to his father, "and not only were my hands and feet cold but my head also began to ache." He felt like going home, but he did not want to offend his hostess and so, rubbing his hands together briskly, he sat down to play. The piano was out of tune and in miserable condition. Yet he played on and against these handicaps did the best he could, hoping to capture the attention of the guests. But the ladies and gentlemen in this cold long hall were busy playing games; they were drawing silly little pictures and were not much interested in Mozart's playing. They talked and laughed among themselves.

Mozart felt that he was playing to the chairs, the tables, and walls. He did not finish the numbers he intended to play, but got up from the piano and made his excuses. He found it impossible to play for people who were so rudely indifferent and lacking in musical understanding.

It was this kind of treatment that prompted him to

write to his father: "Paris is much changed. The French are far from being as polite as they were fifteen years ago. Their manner now borders on rudeness and they are smug."

During this time in Paris Mozart had several pupils and received a commission to compose a ballet. He was also offered the post of organist at Versailles. But the pay was very small, too small, and his friends advised him not to accept.

But if he met many disappointments in Paris, there was one thing which brought him joy. During this time his creative powers had a sudden release. In this he was truly happy. Besides writing the music for the ballet which had been commissioned, he also wrote many other compositions including a symphony and a piano concerto. However, he found it easier to write the music than to get it performed or published.

While in Paris he hoped that he might be commissioned to write an opera. "I must compose a great opera or none. If I write a small one I will receive very little, for here everything is taxed. And if the opera fails to please the public then all is lost, I lose the profit and also my reputation. I must write a great opera because I will then have a greater chance of being appreciated."

Such an opera, Mozart felt, would bring him fame and money so that he would be able to repay his father's debts and bring his father and his sister to

Paris. This was his heart's desire. And he confided to his father: "We will be reunited and all live together in joy and prosperity." But this hope was not to be realized.

One day, quite suddenly, his mother became ill. The doctor came and bled her and left some medicines. At first she seemed a little better, but a few days later she became feverish and delirious. This time the doctor was unable to help her. She died in her son's arms, on July 3.

Mozart feared to send this tragic news home to his father. He wrote to a friend in Salzburg, the Abbé Bullinger, to prepare his father for the shock.

"Mourn with me!" he wrote. "This has been the most melancholy day of my life. I am now writing at two o'clock in the morning. I must tell you that my mother, my darling mother, is no more. God has called her to himself. I clearly see that it was His will to take her from me and I must learn to submit to the will of God. . . . All I would ask of you at present is to act the part of a true friend by preparing my father for this sad news. I have written to him by this post, but only that she is seriously ill. Now I shall wait for your answer and be guided by it."

But when Leopold Mozart received the letter from his son, the letter that was to prepare him for the worst, he already guessed what had happened. He mourned the loss of his wife. She had been the mother of his children and his genial companion for so long that the years ahead now looked dim and empty to him. And he was suddenly possessed with the fear that Wolfgang, although twenty-one years old, was incapable of staying in Paris alone.

Leopold Mozart knew the wonderful qualities of his son, but he also knew of the young man's unworldly traits.

Wolfgang was neither shrewd nor bold and lacked that special coarse quality necessary for success. He was sensitive and had great talent but lacked ability for getting on. He was often outspoken and tactless. He liked to live in the creative world of his imagination and disliked giving lessons or doing routine work, for these things took precious time away from composition and prevented him from writing down the music that was rushing through his mind. His father felt that genius prevented his son from becoming a success.

All these things worried Papa Mozart and made him feel that, perhaps, Wolfgang should come home again. And so he wrote, hoping to soften his son's hatred of Salzburg.

He wrote that it made him sad to learn of all the wonderful music Wolfgang was composing in Paris and which he was longing to hear. He also wrote that the Archbishop now regretted that he had lost Wolfgang's services and might be persuaded to give him a new post in the orchestra, a much better one, one that had recently become vacant and paid well. Besides, there was another orchestra position now vacant which he himself would like to have. One position could perhaps be made dependent on the other. The Archbishop might be persuaded to offer the two positions to them, father and son. They would then receive five hundred florins apiece. This would give them a thousand florins. And with extra lessons and the sale of his *Violin Method* book, the little family would have an income of about one hundred and fifteen florins a month. "In this way," he concluded, "we shall be better off at home than anywhere else where it is twice as dear to live."

To further this involved scheme at the court, Papa Mozart used all his skill. After all, where would the Archbishop find two musicians who were masters in so many fields: musicians who could compose church music, music for festivals, quartets, concertos, and symphonies; who could play the organ and clavier and also lead the violin section of the orchestra; musicians who could rehearse the choirs as well as the orchestra and give lessons in singing, violin, and clavier! This team, father and son, could do all this and take complete charge of the court music.

The Archbishop did not need too much persuasion. He not only offered Papa Mozart and his son the two vacant positions but, also, stipulated that Wolfgang would in a short time again have the title of *Kapellmeister* and that he would allow him to leave Salzburg at any time should he have a commission to do an opera.

Under these generous terms Mozart decided to leave Paris and return to Salzburg. Papa Mozart was happy. For although he knew that Salzburg was narrow and cramped and offered little opportunity for his son's great talent, nevertheless Wolfgang would now again be under his watchful eye.

Papa Mozart had always sheltered his son and taken care of all business matters, and he was certain that Wolfgang, though he was now a grown man, could not manage without him. Papa Mozart imagined that he was a man of the world, shrewd, diplomatic, and a master of all situations. But in reality he was a little man, timid and servile.

However, Wolfgang was a dutiful son. He had always obeyed his father's wishes. He wrote that he was pleased to hear that the Archbishop had consented to allow him to travel when necessary. "Without traveling one becomes a miserable creature. A man of superior talent deteriorates when he remains rooted in one place. If the Archbishop would have confidence in me I would soon make his music famous. My trip to Paris, I assure you, has not been without value. It has helped my composition and also my clavier playing, for now I could not play better. Only one thing I must insist upon in Salzburg and that is that I do not play the violin. I do not want to be a violinist again."

He was through with violin playing forever. He was now a composer and piano virtuoso. And from this time on he never played the violin again in public. He had fallen in love with the new piano, which was a great improvement over the old tinkly clavier. He found the tone of the new piano fuller, richer, and more sustained. This tone seemed to blend better with both string and wind instruments. The action of the hammers was much improved, and the instrument was capable of new and colorful effects. There was much emotional beauty hidden in the keyboard of the new piano, which Wolfgang was eager to explore. It is little wonder he wrote his father that he would never return to the violin again.

And so it was that, in September 1778, Mozart left Paris by slow stage, because it was cheaper, and started back toward Salzburg.

After many tedious days of traveling he arrived in Strasbourg. Here he gave a small concert which brought him much appreciation and applause but only three gold louis in profit, an amount equal to about twelve dollars.

Even though Mozart loved his father and his sister Nannerl and had promised to come home again, still he delayed. Salzburg with its provincial narrowness had become quite hateful to him. And while he had a fairly good position waiting for him, he was unable to forget, or forgive, the constant arrogance and rude-

---

ness of the ignorant Archbishop who had once advised him to go to some school in Italy to learn how to write music! This insult had cut deeply and the wound was still unhealed.

And so, since it was on his way, Mozart decided to stop off at Mannheim, even though he knew that Prince Carl Theodor was no longer there. Some months before, on the death of Maximilian Joseph, the Prince had been elevated to the post of Elector of Bavaria and had moved to Munich with his court and famous orchestra.

Mozart knew this but secretly hoped and prayed that in Mannheim he might still find something to do. The National Theater might give him a commission for an opera or, failing that, a position. Anything to delay his returning to hateful Salzburg!

In the spring of the year he had left Mannheim, with his mother, bound for Paris and fortune. Now it was November of the same year and he was returning alone and empty-handed.

His father had written to hurry home without delay. He had always obeyed his father but now he was determined to stop off at Mannheim. For the first time in his life he did not do exactly as his father wished. He was twenty-two years old and felt he was a grown man and had a right to follow his own judgment, make his own decisions, and lead his own life.

Romance

Mozart's hopes of Mannheim were soon
shattered. There was some talk of his getting a commission from the National
Theater to write music for a drama, but in the end
nothing came of it. After a few weeks he realized
that he was wasting his time.

Nevertheless, his spirits were good. He was in
love. Forgetting his ill-fortune he decided to go to
Munich to see Aloysia Weber, the girl he adored.

Mozart had met Aloysia in the spring when he
and his mother had passed through Mannheim on their
way to Paris. At that time Aloysia was only a little
over fifteen, but she was attractive, tall, slender,
proud, and queenly. And Mozart was instantly captivated by her. Aloysia was a singer with an excellent
soprano voice and one of four daughters. Her father

was a musician and prompter at the Mannheim Opera House. Her mother was a practical woman who was eager to find husbands for her four young daughters. She encouraged Mozart.

Mozart was completely enchanted with Aloysia and was greatly impressed by the rare quality and purity of her voice. He at once sat down and wrote several songs for her. And he dreamed of a time when he and she would be married and would captivate the whole world. He saw before him visions of splendor and glory. He would write wonderful operas and create arias for her which would display her beautiful voice. He would write such music for Aloysia that she would become the most famous prima donna in all the world.

He pictured himself part of the happy Weber family, with Papa Weber and Mamma Weber and the four girls all touring triumphantly through Italy. It would be a glorious time. And he did not forget his own family. They too were included in his dreams.

In almost every letter, he wrote to his father about Aloysia revealing his plans for the future. But Papa Mozart did not share his enthusiasm. He was very worried. He could not see how marrying the beautiful daughter of a penniless musician was going to help Wolfgang's career. And he was greatly relieved when he heard that Wolfgang was leaving for Paris. He hoped that this separation would end the romance.

But time and distance had not cooled Wolfgang's love. He wrote Aloysia long letters from Paris and he continued dreaming of marriage and their future.

Now, less than a year later, he was returning to Munich, where the Webers had moved, and where Aloysia had just been engaged at the Opera House, at a salary of a thousand florins a year. He planned to marry her and he wrote his father telling him so. Papa Mozart did not look forward to sharing his son with anyone, but he no longer objected to Aloysia. Was she not already a prima donna? Was she not now, at sixteen, earning more than he and his talented son together?

But while Papa Mozart did not openly object to the marriage, in his heart he still hoped for a better match. He suggested that Wolfgang delay marriage a while and return at once to Salzburg. The Archbishop was waiting. "All these delays put me in a bad position at court," besides "Salzburg is near Munich and you can visit Aloysia as often as you like." Wolfgang's room was ready for him. "I have secured a good chest where you can keep your clothes and the little clavier is beside your writing table." And then Papa Mozart grew very stern, "I am not able to repay the thousand florins I owe unless my burden is lightened by your aid."

In reply Mozart wrote: "The Archbishop cannot pay me sufficiently for the slavery in his court. And he must no longer attempt to play the great man with me for I know just what he is."

Mozart brushed aside his father's instructions and, leaving Mannheim, went on to Munich, where he believed that all his happiness lay. But he was doomed to bitter disappointment. Aloysia's affections had changed. And she told him that she no longer loved him.

His dream of happiness was broken. He was silent. He could find no words for reply. Sitting at the piano, he expressed his grief in the one way he knew best. He composed a song of sorrow tinged with bitterness.

The next day he left for Salzburg.

In spite of this disappointment, Mozart and Aloysia remained good friends during the years that followed. Mozart wrote a number of songs for her. After she had married an actor named Lange, and had become a famous singer, she created several important roles in some of Mozart's finest operas.

The Break for Freedom

The two and a half years that Mozart spent in Salzburg in the service of the Archbishop were not happy ones. While he was pleased to be home again with his father and Nannerl, he felt that his talents were being wasted. He knew his capabilities and he realized that he was unappreciated. He was no longer the child prodigy who performed like a trained seal. He had grown, he had matured, and he was aware of the creative powers burning within himself. He knew he could match and even excel the best that was being produced in Europe.

His routine labors at the Archbishop's court filled most of his time. It was work that others could have done, and Mozart felt that much of it was degrading. He also resented the time it took; time which he would have liked to spend in composing. He did, however, manage to do some work of his own in his spare hours. With his usual energy he wrote, among other things, four symphonies, six piano sonatas, and two concertos. He also wrote some incidental music for a drama entitled *Thamos, King of Egypt*. This work was quite important for it paved the way for one of his great masterpieces, *The Magic Flute*.

Mozart's routine duties for the Archbishop were pleasantly interrupted one day by the good news that the new Elector of Bavaria, Carl Theodor, had at last decided to give him a commission to do an opera. The libretto chosen for this opera was *Idomeneo*, a story from Greek mythology.

Mozart was very happy because this meant a few weeks of freedom. His agreement with the Archbishop clearly stated that he would be allowed to leave Salzburg if he should get a commission to write an opera. Besides, to have the opportunity of writing music for the Elector Carl Theodor's wonderful orchestra, one of the finest in all Europe, was the fulfillment of a cherished dream. He was inspired to feverish creative energy.

He worked with fury and in three months' time *Idomeneo*, his first dramatic masterpiece, was completed. The autograph score filled 458 pages of music paper. Even before it was completed Mozart ran off to Munich to get the first act into rehearsal.

The last rehearsal of *Idomeneo* took place on Mozart's twenty-fifth birthday, January 27, 1781. And two days later the curtain went up on the first performance. *Idomeneo* was, from the start, a brilliant success. It is one of Mozart's most ambitious operas.

The happy time of rehearsing this new opera and working with the famous orchestra was soon over. However, Mozart tarried on at Munich, enjoying the pleasures of the carnival season. The Archbishop, who had been impressed with the success of his servant, suddenly summoned Mozart to join him in Vienna. The Empress Maria Theresa had recently died and her son Joseph had mounted the throne; the Archbishop of Salzburg had decided to go to Vienna to pay his respects to the new ruler.

The Archbishop traveled with a retinue. Besides his courtiers he took along some household servants, two cooks, a confectioner, an exchequer, and two valets. And so that he might entertain the Viennese nobility he brought along his private composer and virtuoso. If the Elector of Bavaria, Carl Theodor, thought well enough of Mozart to ask him to write an opera, then the composer was certainly good enough to be displayed along with the special confectioner and cooks.

Mozart was pleased to go to Vienna where he was certain his music would be understood and appreciated. But rudeness and lack of consideration on the part of his overbearing master soon began to anger him. The Archbishop made strict conditions. Mozart was required to eat at the table with the servants. The valets sat at the head of the table. Mozart's place was beneath the valets but above the cooks. This was humiliating enough, but the Archbishop imposed other conditions. He would not permit Mozart to give public concerts, nor would he allow him to accept invitations to play for friends among the Viennese nobility. The Archbishop insisted that Mozart be on hand twenty-four hours a day in case he felt in the mood for a little music.

Mozart knew that the Emperor Joseph was a lover of music, and he was eager to play for him. There were friends in Vienna who were ready to bring him to the palace. But the Archbishop would not hear of such a thing.

Mozart resented the pettiness of his master and wrote to his father: "I did not know I was a valet and this is my ruin. I am expected to loiter every morning for a couple of hours in the anteroom. . . . I did not understand that this would be part of my duties. However I always come promptly when the Archbishop summons me." Then he added that he would much rather work for another man at half pay than for such a man as the Archbishop. And he begged his father not to write him again about being dutiful and obedient in the face of such humiliating treatment.

Mozart was not the only one who disliked the Archbishop. The Emperor Joseph was diplomatic and accepted homage from the Archbishop of Salzburg, but he did not invite him to his summer palace, although he invited almost all the others who had come to pay their respects. The Archbishop considered this an insult and in anger he ordered his household, confectioner, cooks, valets, and private composer, to return immediately to Salzburg.

Mozart, however, was unable to leave at once and he reported this fact to the angry Archbishop.

"I planned to leave tonight but the coach is full and I cannot get a seat," he explained.

"There, I knew it! No one serves me so badly. I should stop your salary. Why must I pay out money to ragamuffins and scamps and rogues!"

These angry words led to others. On the following day Mozart wrote another letter of resignation. Thus ended his services with the Archbishop.

He wrote his father the full details of this quarrel and added: "I don't want to have anything more to do with Salzburg. I hate the Archbishop to madness." And he begged his father to understand all the insults that he had been forced to endure. Besides, Vienna was a wonderful place. It would be good for him to remain there for then he would be free to work out his own musical destiny. In Vienna where music was loved and understood, he had many friends and he could foresee endless opportunities. In fact he already had prospects. Then he added: "I shall send you by the next post a little money and this I hope will convince you that in Vienna I will not starve."

Mozart feared that his father would not approve of his having left the services of the Archbishop, and would want him to come home to Salzburg. He knew that, even though he was twenty-five years old, his father still regarded him as a little boy, incapable of looking after himself. He knew all these things, yet he trusted that his father would understand as he always had in the past. And he was shocked to find that his father not only disapproved completely of his actions but even sided with the Archbishop.

Every post brought Mozart another long letter voicing his father's displeasure. He even suggested that Mozart reconsider his rash action, apologize to the Archbishop, and ask to be taken back!

Wolfgang tried desperately to explain his feelings. In one letter he wrote: "The things which the Archbishop said to me . . . the language used by this truly worthy man of God, had such a physical effect on me that in the evening at the opera, in the middle of the first act, I had to go home and lie down, for I was feverish, trembled in every limb and staggered along the street like a drunkard. . . ."

But Papa Mozart did not understand. And the failure of his father to support him at this crucial time upset Mozart very much. He had always placed so much trust and confidence in his father: now he felt deserted. Yet he knew that in no circumstances could he return to Salzburg. His sensitive nature could no longer endure bondage. Vienna was to him freedom.

The bitterness that marked this dispute between father and son was never forgotten. But Mozart was determined to liberate himself at any cost, even at the painful price of losing his father's love.

Vienna and Marriage

Mozart lived only ten years after leaving the Archbishop. Vienna became his home. And although these years were troubled with poverty and disappointments, he was free.

This freedom gave wing and glory to Mozart's creative powers. Music flowed from his pen without interruption, without restraint. He was free to express his musical ideas in any way he liked. And he poured out the hidden joys and sorrows of his heart in a great variety of compositions. During these years his work reached full maturity. Almost everything he wrote at this time is a masterpiece. Every composition is charged with a high quality of musical invention; it is balanced, sensitive, and inspiring.

This was the period when Mozart's musical genius reached its full greatness and marked him as one of the world's supreme masters. He drew his emotional inspiration from the deep lonely heart of man. This heart he understood because he himself had so often been rejected, brushed aside, treated with rude indifference, and insulted. His sensitive nature felt all such things very deeply. His creative powers gave expression to these feelings, to the dark shadows of life. And free Vienna, together with his sunny nature, gave his music the necessary contrasting color and gaiety.

It was during these years that Mozart, liberated from the hateful Archbishop and provincial Salzburg, was able to allow his imagination to take wing. Freedom and imagination are necessary for creative work. And the compositions of this Vienna period made Mozart immortal.

All Vienna recognized the genius in their midst and made Mozart feel welcome. He renewed old friendships and tried to find pupils.

He was at length successful and wrote his father: "I have one pupil at present, the Countess Rumbeck. I could certainly have many more if I lowered my fee. . . . My terms are six ducats for twelve lessons. . . . I would rather have three people who pay me well than six who pay poorly. By means of this one pupil I can just manage and that is enough for the present." Six ducats for twelve lessons would come to about a dollar a lesson in our present currency. Yet he wanted his father to know he could manage with this small sum and that he was content. Poverty and freedom in Vienna he considered better than security in Salzburg.

It was not long before he found other pupils. The Countess Thun, who was a distinguished musician, and her son-in-law, Prince Lichnowsky, came to study with him. The Prince was a special friend of music and musicians. Some years later Beethoven, in gratitude, dedicated several of his compositions to this man.

Two other members of Vienna society were at this time attracted to Mozart. One was the Russian Ambassador, Prince Galitzin, and the other the gay and influential Baroness von Waldstadten. Prince Galitzin engaged Mozart to play the piano at all his private recitals. He always sent his carriage for him. And the brilliant Baroness was the first in Vienna to take Mozart under her wing. In spite of the fact that Mozart described her as a very "flighty person and as variable as the wind" she was kind, generous, and good. And later, in times of difficulty, Mozart was often able to turn to her for sympathy and help.

Mozart was also favored by a certain Baron van Swieten. Every Sunday afternoon he and other musicians gathered at this nobleman's home. "Here nothing is played but Handel and Johann Sebastian Bach. And I am now making a collection of the Bach fugues," he wrote to his father.

This is a most significant line for here we learn that

Mozart was the first to collect Bach's fugues. Bach had been dead for thirty-two years and very few of his compositions had been published. His music was unpopular; its grandeur was not recognized by the public until many years later. Yet at this early date Mozart understood Bach's greatness. In this he was far ahead of his time.

During these same early days in Vienna, Mozart was happy to learn that the Emperor Joseph II held chamber concerts in his private apartments every afternoon. Unfortunately, the Emperor preferred Italian music, and it was only with difficulty that the good Countess Thun was finally able to persuade him to have some of Mozart's music performed.

In time, however, the Emperor grew to like Mozart's music and before many months had passed he gave him a commission to do an opera. Nothing could have pleased Mozart more. The libretto which was chosen had a Turkish background because Turkish themes and music with Turkish characters were very popular at that period. It was entitled *The Abduction from the Seraglio* and was a comedy. Mozart set to work at once with great pleasure. The work was to be composed and performed for the Grand Duke Paul of Russia who was due to visit Vienna in a few months' time.

The first performance of *The Abduction from the Seraglio* took place on the night of July 16, 1782. It was received with rapture and in the months that followed was repeated many times to filled houses.

Mozart was further honored during the visit of the Russian Grand Duke. He was invited to appear at court and take part in a piano-playing contest with the Italian virtuoso Clementi. The Emperor, his royal guests, the Grand Duke and Duchess, and the entire court were present.

The Emperor privately favored Mozart and he laid a wager with the Russian Grand Duchess that Mozart would prove superior.

When all were assembled and comfortably settled, the Emperor ordered Clementi to begin. The Italian virtuoso played a prelude and a sonata. Mozart listened carefully, and at once recognized Clementi's great facility. He thought the Italian's right hand very well developed and considered the man's greatest achievement his passages in thirds. But Mozart felt that Clementi was a mere machine and played without taste or feeling.

When Clementi had finished the sonata, the Emperor turned to Mozart and said very informally: "Come, now, fire away!" Mozart began with a prelude and then played a theme with variations.

After Mozart was finished, the Grand Duchess of Russia handed each performer the manuscript of a sonata. Mozart played one part and Clementi another. Then for the further amusement of the audience the Emperor gave the two musicians a theme which they proceeded to develop on two pianos, alternately accompanying one another.

When this informal contest was over, the Emperor was very pleased with Mozart. He complimented him in private. The Russian Grand Duchess was forced to admit that Mozart was superior. She paid the wager.

It is because of this contest that we today have a description of Mozart's playing as evaluated by a piano virtuoso. Writing to a friend soon after the affair, Clementi described Mozart's playing in the following words: "I had until this time never heard piano playing which was so full of spirit and grace. I was most delighted with an Adagio and with several of Mozart's extemporized variations which he made on a theme given him by the Emperor."

By "spirit" Clementi meant tonal quality, precision, and contrast. By "grace" he meant phrasing, expression, and intelligence. Mechanical playing is wholly lacking in feeling and intelligence.

During these happy first months in Vienna Mozart roomed with his friends the Webers. They had recently moved from Munich to Vienna.

Aloysia, his first love, was now married to a handsome actor named Lange. Her place in Mozart's affections was now taken by a younger sister, Constanze.

It was with great hesitation that Mozart wrote to his father about Constanze, for he again feared disapproval. "My disposition has always inclined me to domestic life," he wrote. "I have never from my youth been able to take care of my linen or clothes and other things and therefore I think it would be well if I could find a wife. How many little extra expenses I would save! An unmarried man, in my opinion, enjoys only half a life. But now who is the object of my love? Do not be startled, I beg. Not one of the Webers, surely? Yes, one of the Webers. It is the third eldest and beloved Constanze who is the martyr of the family and who is the kindest and cleverest and in short the very best of them all. . . . I must make you better acquainted with the character of my Constanze. She is not plain but at the same time she is far from being handsome. Her great beauty consists in a pair of sparkling black eyes and a pretty figure. She is not witty, but has enough good sense to enable her to fulfill her duties as a wife and mother. Her dress is always neat and she can make most of her clothes herself. She dresses her own hair, understands housekeeping and has the best heart in all the world. I love her with my whole soul, as she does me. Tell me if I could wish for a better wife."

With these words Mozart hoped to gain his father's approval and consent. But his father did not think that the daughter of a "poor shiftless musician," badly educated and not at all good looking, would be any advantage to his son. Constanze's sister Aloysia had been a different matter; she was already a prima donna and had the promise of a brilliant future. Besides he did not like the Weber family and knew the mother to be "very crafty and a heavy drinker," and his son "quite innocent in the ways of the world."

Papa Mozart was very much upset by Wolfgang's letter, for he felt that marriage without an assured income could only lead to misery and ruin. He considered his son's optimistic outlook the result of dreaming. He felt that if Wolfgang married a girl like Constanze, his prospects for the future would not be good.

For these reasons Papa Mozart withheld his consent. He also secretly hoped that his son's infatuation with Constanze was a passing fancy. But it was not. Mozart loved her and wrote again and again begging for his father's permission.

For a second time in Mozart's adult life, his father failed him. He had refused, only a short time before, to understand Wolfgang's need for freedom from the Archbishop; he now objected to his son's marriage and withheld his consent. And this time, as before, Mozart was forced to go ahead on his own. He and Constanze were married on August 4, 1782.

When Papa Mozart realized that Wolfgang was going to marry Constanze anyway, he sat down and quickly wrote a letter giving his consent. The letter arrived a day after the wedding.

From this moment on Mozart felt that his father no

longer understood him. He never got over the fact that his own father wanted to prevent his happiness. However, he hoped that perhaps some day when his father met Constanze he would understand and change his mind.

Papa Mozart, on the other hand, was deeply wounded by his son's independence. He had brought him up to be obedient and had done everything possible for him. Now he felt he must resign the charge and let God guide Wolfgang. "I have done my duty as a father," he said in resignation.

The correspondence between father and son became less frequent and the tone of their letters quite cool. This strained relationship worried Mozart greatly, for he loved his father dearly. He clung to the hope that if his father could meet and know Constanze, he would see her virtues and understand what a good wife she was.

In an effort to heal this bitter estrangement Mozart decided to take his wife on a visit to his old home in Salzburg. For three months in the summer of 1783 the family were together. Things went along fairly well. Papa Mozart accepted his daughter-in-law to some degree.

It was during these months that Mozart worked on a great Mass in C Minor that he had begun earlier the same year. Four sections were performed in the Salzburg Cathedral and Constanze, whose voice was thin and pale compared to her sister's, sang the soprano solos. This is her only recorded public appearance as a performer.

This great C Minor Mass was very different from the trivial church music that Mozart had written at the order of the hateful Archbishop. When the first notes were sounded on the organ all Salzburg realized that they were in the presence of an inspired work of art. The Mass was charged with religious fervor. Mozart said that he had written it with deep emotional feeling and in gratitude to God for his marriage to Constanze.

During these same three months in Salzburg Mozart once more began experimenting with dramatic musical composition. And it was these experiments that foreshadowed the style, a few years later, of *Figaro* and *Don Giovanni,* two Mozart operas that have since become world famous.

Thus, the time in Salzburg was most productive even though it failed to establish the friendly relations Mozart had hoped for between his father and Constanze. Mozart's marriage to her had caused a family rift which could never be healed.

Returning to Vienna, Mozart wrote his father thanking him for a wonderful long visit. But the letter was formal and reflected their strained relationship.

Settled once more in Vienna with Constanze, Mozart found that life was not easy. It proved very difficult to earn a living with lessons and concerts.

When Papa Mozart heard that Wolfgang was thinking of leaving Vienna to try his fortune in Paris or London, he wrote to a friend: "I see great faults in my son. He is too indolent and easy-going and at times he is even too proud. Such traits make a man inactive. He is also most impatient and is often ruled by extreme opposites. Either he has too much or too little. There is never a middle way with him."

The father apparently failed to understand that a creative artist is impelled by an inner force to give expression to that which is pressing at his heart, regardless of money. He also failed to understand that it is natural for a true artist to have "too much or too little." And he was quite wrong in accusing a genius like Wolfgang of being indolent. No one could have worked harder or produced more. The amount of work Mozart turned out in the last eight years of his life is staggering. And the quality of this work is supreme. Yet the total sum he earned from these compositions was not enough to support him and his family, and he was always forced to supplement this income with concerts and lessons.

A patron would have solved this problem and relieved Mozart's financial pressure. He never stopped hoping that he might attract a worthy patron or find temporary employment with a rich count or duke, or even the Emperor himself.

Yes, there were often rumors in Vienna that the

Emperor looked upon Mozart with favor and was about to take him into his service. These rumors even reached Papa Mozart in Salzburg. But Mozart always had to write to say that nothing definite had been proposed. He repeatedly wrote in this manner: "Though it is a fact that the whole town talks of it, and a number of people have already congratulated me and I know it has been mentioned in the Emperor's presence. . . . Matters are so far advanced that the Emperor has it in his head. . . . The affair has gone so far without any application on my part. . . . Were I to stir in the matter and appear anxious I would then get a smaller salary for the Emperor is known to be very stingy."

Yes, the Emperor was stingy, and he was also inconsiderate. Year after year he allowed the rumors to circulate throughout musical Vienna, and he allowed Mozart to keep on hoping. And when he finally did do something, it was very little indeed.

The hope for a post in the Emperor's service was ever before Mozart. In the meantime he earned his living giving lessons and selling tickets for his subscription concerts. He himself described his typical day in these words: "I pass the forenoons in giving lessons until two o'clock, when we dine. In the afternoons there are more lessons. The evening is therefore the only time I have for composing, and even that is by no means certain for I am often invited to concerts. There are still two concertos to be written for my subscription concerts."

Even so, in the little time Mozart had for composing, he accomplished a great deal. He wrote rapidly and with great certainty. He seldom needed to revise or correct a line. And it is most surprising that his compositions, produced under the extreme pressure of existence and executed so rapidly, show no signs of carelessness or looseness of musical structure. Never does he falter in his thematic development and never once does he lose sight of musical balance and the quality and tone of the instruments. His musical ideas are complete. He made no rough sketches, no first drafts, and no corrected copies. Each composition was, from the very first, a finished and unified whole.

Mozart's mind was ever filled with original music. Before he wrote a single note on paper his compositions were completely finished in his thoughts. The actual writing was almost like copying something that was already in existence.

During the process of writing down what was already organized in his mind, Mozart was not disturbed by anything that went on around him. In fact, at such times, he liked to have his wife sit beside him chatting away and telling him funny stories. Once he wrote part of one of his great operas in the garden of a friend while he and some other guests were playing quoits. He would jump up from the table where he was writing to take his turn at the game. At other times, while playing billiards and waiting for an opponent to complete his shots, Mozart would write out pages and pages of music. Occasionally, while putting one composition on paper, his mind would be busy creating another. In a letter to his sister he once confessed that he thought out a prelude while writing down a fugue.

This seems all the more remarkable when one realizes that it was not only the melody, harmony, and counterpoint that he carried in his mind but also the parts for every instrument in the orchestra! Often his big sheets of music paper, ruled for twelve parts, were not large enough. To express his musical ideas he sometimes had to attach extra paper with five or six more lines for additional instruments. Mozart was living in the age when music was expanding, when orchestras were growing and becoming more colorful. And he did much to aid this musical development and pave the way for that liberation which Beethoven was to accomplish a generation later.

While Mozart wrote easily, rapidly, and faultlessly, and had the self-confidence of genius, he was not indifferent to his finished work. Without excess vanity he had always felt that his work had value, but now he began to recognize its unique qualities. He began to feel that his work was a contribution to musical literature. He knew that it had reached maturity. And while in the past he had kept no record of his compositions, nor listed their opus numbers, he now, in the year 1784, began keeping a book in which he listed each composition, its themes, its key, and the date when it was finished.

In the seven years that remained of his life, Mozart was able to list in this book over two hundred works, some of them long symphonies, concertos, and operas. And as we already know, many of these compositions, some of which have become immortal, were written at night after the day's lessons and concert playing!

It was during Mozart's years in Vienna that a genuine friendship developed between him and Haydn. This friendship existed even though Haydn was twenty-four years older than Mozart. It was never marred by jealousy even though Haydn lived in comfort and Mozart lived in dire poverty.

Haydn had the good fortune to be employed by a kindly and appreciative Hungarian prince named Esterhazy, who was fabulously wealthy. Here, in the comfort and protection of the prince's palace, Haydn was able to pursue his art in tranquillity, free from the fear of poverty. He did not have to interrupt his creative flight with tedious lessons on the piano and with concert appearances. Yet Haydn's comfort and security did not lessen his industry. Nor did it cheapen his art.

Even more remarkable is the fact that poverty and insecurity did not force Mozart to lower the quality of his work and compromise with the musical taste of his day. When a music publisher ordered him to write in a more popular vein if he wanted to be published, Mozart replied: "Then may the devil take me, for I will write nothing more. I would rather go hungry."

Both Haydn and Mozart were artists of extreme integrity, and each respected the other. There was no rivalry between them. They often met together to try out new music. In many ways they encouraged each other.

Mozart learned a great deal about the writing of quartets from Haydn. And to acknowledge this debt he wrote a set of six quartets, masterpieces, which he dedicated with these words: "To my dear friend Haydn: A father having resolved to send forth his children into the wide world is anxious to entrust them to the protection and guidance of a man who enjoys much celebrity there and who fortunately is moreover his best friend. Here then are the children I entrust to a man so renowned, and so dear to me. . . . During your last stay in Vienna you yourself, my dearest friend, expressed your satisfaction with them. . . . Be pleased then to receive them kindly and to be to them a father, a guide and a friend. . . . I am from my heart your sincere friend, Mozart."

But while Mozart learned from Haydn, Haydn also

learned from Mozart. He studied Mozart's compositions and found in them a new and wonderful freedom
which he admired greatly. Their rich harmonies and
the creative imagination which they contained captivated him. And these qualities, which we now know
as Mozartean, Haydn expressed in the work of his
later years.

Haydn also loved to listen to Mozart's playing, the
extreme beauty of which, he said many years later,
was haunting and quite unforgettable. And he attended as many of his concerts as he could.

So highly did Haydn regard Mozart that he once
said to Papa Mozart: "I tell you before God and as a
man of honor, that your son is the greatest composer
of whom I have ever heard. He not only has taste but
in addition he has the most complete knowledge of
composition."

1784   1787

Figaro *and Prague*

While living in Vienna, Mozart was fortunate enough to meet an Italian poet and former school teacher named Lorenzo da Ponte. This man came from Venice. Here he had published stories and satires which brought him notoriety but made him so many enemies that he had been forced to flee.

Arriving in Vienna, Lorenzo da Ponte succeeded in obtaining the position of poet to the royal theater. He was at once attracted to Mozart's music and proposed that they collaborate on an opera. Da Ponte agreed to provide the dramatic libretto if Mozart would write the music.

This suggestion was very pleasing to Mozart. He felt that his former operas had all suffered because of their poor librettos. If only he had a good poem, then he was sure he could write an opera which would captivate the world. Da Ponte, he felt, was the man.

The work that Mozart and Da Ponte undertook to make into an opera was a French play by Beaumarchais entitled *The Marriage of Figaro*. It had been produced in Paris about a year before. Beaumarchais had been an ardent supporter of the American Revolution and when *The Marriage of Figaro* was produced it created a sensation. It was frankly outspoken and revolutionary in tone. Because of this it had shocked the French King, Louis XVI, and he had ordered it banned.

But the French public cried aloud and demanded that the play be continued. And since even the Queen, Marie Antoinette, liked the play, the King finally gave in and allowed it to return to the stage. The public welcomed the reopening with feverish enthusiasm.

All this took place five years before the outbreak of the French Revolution. The American Revolution had already been fought and won, and hope of a new kind of freedom was in the air. The stormy career of this play gives a clear indication of how the political wind was blowing.

Mozart was not in the least politically minded but he liked the idea of *The Marriage of Figaro* and was eager to get to work. However, when the Emperor Joseph II heard of this, he forbade it. He refused to give his consent until Da Ponte was able to assure him that the story would be cleansed of any objectionable political allusions. Emperor Joseph was, after all, Marie Antoinette's elder brother and Louis XVI was his brother-in-law.

The composition of *Figaro* was begun in the fall of 1785 and finished in the spring of the following year.

Da Ponte wrote the lines of the libretto rapidly. As fast as they were written Mozart composed the music. Da Ponte recognized the genius of Mozart, his musical ability as well as his wonderful dramatic feeling, and had the good sense to follow many of Mozart's suggestions.

As soon as the opera was completed Da Ponte took it himself to the Emperor. Once more he assured his Majesty that the opera contained no objectionable matter. In fact, he said, the characters were quite different from those in the French play; Mozart had changed them to fit his own whimsical personality and the extremely beautiful music he had written. The Emperor was gracious enough to accept Da Ponte's word and ordered the opera to be put into rehearsal without delay.

The performers were all Italian, except for an Irish tenor named Michael Kelly and an English soprano, Nancy Storace. All had excellent voices. Mozart himself took charge of the rehearsals and coached the singers in their special roles.

For the opening performance, which took place on the first of May, 1786, Mozart, dressed in his best, appeared in the orchestra pit and conducted from the keyboard. He was happy with anticipation and his face was radiant. Michael Kelly has left us a description of Mozart on this memorable night. "His little animated countenance lighted up with the glowing rays of genius, as impossible to describe as it would be to paint sunbeams."

The opera house was full, and as soon as the very first notes of the overture were sounded the audience fell under the spell of the music. All were aware that they were in the presence of a great work of art.

Each aria was applauded loudly, and so many numbers had to be repeated that the opera lasted nearly twice its appointed time. But the success was not lasting. A strong clique of envious and embittered musicians and composers worked against Mozart. These men recognized Mozart's genius only too well and it galled them. They found many excuses for bolstering their prejudice: they said he was too outspoken and too independent. There was much intrigue between the Emperor's palace and the opera house. And there were other operas, other musical novelties that the public was anxious to hear.

So there were only nine performances of *Figaro* in eight months. Mozart was so discouraged that he decided never again to produce an opera in Vienna.

· · ·

129

Mozart received nothing for the nine performances of *Figaro* because he had been paid a lump sum in advance and this had not yet been made up. He had hoped that *Figaro* would be a financial success and thus lighten the burden of his debts. But he now found himself worse off than before.

Constanze was sick. Their first-born son had died in infancy. Their second son Carl was two years old. They were paying too much rent for their first-floor apartment. Because of Mozart's lessons to members of the nobility he felt he needed a respectable place to live. He was, therefore, saddled with high rent he found difficult to pay. Added to these troubles in Vienna, he had just received the news that his father was quite ill in Salzburg.

About a month later news reached Mozart that his father had died on May 28, 1787. Although their relationship had in recent years become strained, Mozart felt this loss very deeply. His father had meant a great deal to him; they had been together for so many years. His whole life had been molded by his father.

Mozart was now thirty-one years old. The death of his father, the failure of *Figaro*, which in his heart he knew was a masterpiece, and his mounting debts made him feel he would never attain worldly success, not even in music-loving Vienna. It was true, he admitted, that there were some in Vienna who understood and appreciated his music. But they were only a few. Mozart's dreams of gaining public acclaim, of finding a patron, or of winning the Emperor's favor faded away. He was now convinced that he would have to work on alone and unwanted.

This sad realization, which came to Mozart at the age of thirty-one, brought about a change in his character. From this time on he seemed resigned to fate. He accepted failure as part of his lot. And he often acted as though he were a man doomed.

Yet in the face of such deep discouragement he did not abandon his music. Neither success nor failure could stem the miraculous flow of music. He mastered his bitterness and discouragement so successfully that, in the years that followed, his music reached even greater heights than before. Some of his finest masterpieces were still to come. How creation could have gone on in such circumstances remains a wonder!

But suddenly through the blackness of this night there shone a golden ray of sunlight. Good news came from Prague.

Figaro was produced in Prague, the capital of Czechoslovakia (then known as Bohemia). It was a tremendous success. Night after night great crowds of excited music lovers flocked to the opera house. This was music that they understood. It filled their hearts and they carried the tunes away with them.

They sang many of the arias on the streets; even begging musicians played snatches from *Figaro* to attract crowds and collect pennies.

Mozart was invited by Count Thun, the father-in-law of his pupil and friend the Countess Thun, to come to Prague and bask in this rare sunshine. When he arrived at the opera house the news of his presence was quickly whispered about. As soon as the overture ended the audience rose and cheered him. Again and again he bowed to acknowledge the resounding cries *Viva Maestro!*

When the opera was over the musicians flocked about Mozart and said that they were so enthusiastic about the music that even now, at midnight, they could begin all over again. Some days later he wrote to a friend in Vienna that he had attended a ball "where the flower of Prague beauties were assembled. . . . And here they danced with the greatest pleasure to the music from my *Figaro*, for many of the arias have been transcribed into quadrilles and waltzes. For in the city of Prague nothing is talked about but *Figaro*, nothing is played but *Figaro*, nothing whistled or sung in the streets but *Figaro*, no opera so crowded as *Figaro*, everywhere everything is *Figaro*. All this is indeed very flattering to me."

Here at last, in Prague, Mozart had found genuine appreciation.

Later Mozart gave a public concert in the opera house at Prague. The house was full. The program consisted entirely of his own music. At the end of the concert the ovation was so great that he had to play numerous encores. One of these was a set of variations which he improvised on the popular airs from *Figaro*.

Elated with this great success, Mozart decided to write another opera. Some months before, he had resolved never again to produce an opera in Vienna and he held firm to this vow. His new opera would be for the people of Prague. These were the only people in all Europe, he felt, who really understood and appreciated him.

Before leaving Prague, he signed a contract with the manager of the opera house to write an opera next season for a fee of a hundred ducats.

Returning to Vienna, Mozart consulted at once with Da Ponte about a new libretto. The Italian poet had a good suggestion. He proposed that they take the adventures of the famous Don Juan and work them into an opera. In this way was born the masterpiece that we know today by the name *Don Giovanni*.

It is interesting to note that about a month before Mozart left Prague and before he had the contract for his new opera, Joseph Haydn had been asked to write an opera for the Prague Opera House. He refused, saying that all his work was done for Prince Esterhazy's own company in Hungary. Then with true loyalty and full sincerity he added: "It would be a risk since one can hardly compete with the great Mozart. It wish I could impress in the heart of every music lover, especially the great, how wonderful are the works of Mozart. And if they could feel them as deeply and with such musical understanding as I myself feel them, then nations would compete with each other to gain possession of so precious a jewel. Prague must hold on to this rare man and should also reward him, otherwise the life of a great genius is a sad one. . . . How many hopeful spirits have gone under! I am indignant that this rare Mozart has as yet not found employment with any imperial or royal court."

While this letter may have added weight, especially since it came from Joseph Haydn, it was really the enthusiasm of the people of Prague that secured for Mozart the contract for the new opera.

But this letter is significant, for it shows the great friendship and understanding of a fellow creative artist; it was an earnest plea for Mozart's recognition.

Genius should be rewarded. "How many hopeful spirits have gone under!" With these words Haydn showed that he understood and that he feared for Mozart's future.

The Full Flowering

The romantic story of Don Juan, so rich in dramatic possibilities, set Mozart's creative powers aflame. The music began to take shape in his mind and by the time Da Ponte had completed his libretto, Mozart already had the opera well advanced.

However, work on *Don Giovanni* did not prevent Mozart from composing other music. He found time in the spring of this same year, 1787, to write two of his most beautiful quintets which he scored for two violins, two violas, and a cello. And in August, when *Don Giovanni* was already well in hand, he paused long enough to write out the famous serenade which he himself called *Eine kleine Nachtmusik* ("A little night music"). This work, because of its beautiful melodies, is considered one of the world's great musical masterpieces. For a century and a half it has delighted our hearts.

During this spring, while Mozart was working on *Don Giovanni*, an interesting incident occurred which cannot go unrecorded. He received a visit from a young German musician. The youth was seventeen years old, thick-set, with a pock-marked face, and had the heavy accent which indicated that he came from the Rhine country.

The visitor said he had been attracted to Mozart's playing and would like very much to take a few lessons during his brief visit to Vienna.

Mozart asked the rough-looking young man to go to the piano and play something, anything at all. He expected to hear the conventional, meaningless piano playing of the day, but from the very first chord was delightfully surprised.

There were others present in the room, and when the young man finished Mozart turned to them and said: "This young man should be watched. He will soon make a noise in the world." Then he turned to the youth and asked: "Please tell us again, what is your name?"

"My name is Ludwig van Beethoven."

In September Mozart, accompanied by his wife, journeyed to Prague for the second time. But *Don*

Giovanni was still far from finished, or rather, though most of it was clear in Mozart's mind, a good part had yet to be written out. This Mozart did while sitting in the summerhouse of a friend's garden, from which he had a fine view of the old city of Prague. He wrote rapidly. He was certain of every note. In a few weeks the bulk of the manuscript pages were ready for the copyists. Once they were copied rehearsals began.

The rehearsals got underway in the middle of October, and the opera was scheduled to open at the end of the same month. During these two weeks all the orchestra parts and all the singers' arias had to be whipped into shape. It was a lot of work, but it was rewarding. Mozart was happy.

In spite of all this labor, however, the opera was not yet complete. On the night before the opening, the overture had still to be written out. But this did not worry Mozart for he had it all clearly composed in his head.

That night he and his wife had supper at the home of some friends. It was a leisurely, pleasant evening and Mozart sat at the piano and composed a song for his hostess. When the song was finished a friend reminded Mozart that in twenty-four hours the curtain would be going up on his new opera *Don Giovanni* and that the overture was still not written! "It will be done at once," he said, and leaving the company, he went up to his room.

He asked Constanze to mix him a bowl of punch

and to sit beside him and tell him fairy-tales while he wrote out the score for the orchestra. The punch he felt would be pleasant and the fairy-tales would prevent him from falling asleep.

But the punch made him drowsy and Constanze was forced to tell him one tale after another to keep him awake.

By sunrise the pages were ready to be sent to the copyists who, because of the delay, were forced to work at feverish speed in order to have all the orchestra parts ready for that afternoon. No rehearsal was possible, for there was no time. Mozart paid the musicians a great compliment by saying that the Prague orchestra, he was confident, could play a new overture at sight without a rehearsal.

They did. And it all sounded very wonderful even if a good many notes "dropped below the desk" and a few others were not played correctly. But since Mozart was conducting from the piano he indicated each tempo and, fortifying the melodic line, made it easier for the orchestra. No one in the audience knew that the orchestra was trying to read this difficult music at sight.

Don Giovanni was a brilliant success. The warm-hearted people of Prague were most enthusiastic. In one week the opera was repeated three times and the manager of the opera house told Da Ponte that as long as he and Mozart continued working together the

Prague opera house would never have a bad season. Popular favor was guarantee of success.

This second visit to Prague marks the height of Mozart's worldly success. He was never again to attain such public approval. Returning to Vienna he found the atmosphere very different.

Hearing of the phenomenal success of *Don Giovanni* in Prague, some of Mozart's friends had proposed that the opera be produced in Vienna. But the same old envious and powerful cliques, led by embittered rivals, did their very best to prevent this. The intrigues were so great that at length they reached the Emperor's ears. This time he grew weary of all the endless backbiting and commanded that the opera be put into rehearsal at once.

Several years before, Mozart had vowed that he would never again allow one of his operas to be produced in Vienna, and it was not long before he had reason to regret that he had weakened in this resolve. His masterpiece, which had enjoyed such success in Prague, was not appreciated in Vienna, and failed on its opening night.

The next day the members of the company began suggesting remedies. Most of the singers insisted on extra numbers to display their special talents. Mozart foolishly gave in and inserted several pieces into his original work. Composed at a different time and in a different mood, none of these fit logically into the opera. Aloysia Lange (his sister-in-law and the girl he had once loved) and two other singers were the only ones who understood the quality of the original work and did not demand any changes.

The revised opera did not succeed any better. It was produced only fifteen times in the course of the year. The music did not please the average opera goers who, as a critic of the day observed, "liked to have their ears tickled rather than have their hearts moved."

Mozart, however, did have one consolation, for Emperor Joseph II admired the opera and was disappointed at its reception. He said: "The opera is divine, perhaps even more beautiful than *Figaro*, but no food for the teeth of my Viennese."

And Mozart, with full confidence and faith that his work would someday be appreciated, answered: "Let us give them time to chew it."

At about this same time Emperor Joseph II gave Mozart another grain of consolation. Upon the death of the court composer, Gluck, at the age of seventy-three, Mozart was appointed to this coveted post.

Mozart had long been seeking and dreaming of a position at the royal court. Its steady income would, he thought, relieve the pressures of his existence. But now that his wish had come true it proved to be just one more disappointment. However kind and friendly the Emperor was to Mozart he still retained his pettiness. Gluck's salary had been two thousand florins a year, but Mozart for the same position was to be paid only eight hundred florins, or about four hundred dollars! And for this the Emperor kept him busy writing popular minuets and waltzes for the palace balls. His full talents were never called upon.

No wonder that Mozart, in signing one of the receipts for his pay, added the words: "Too much for what I do. And too little for what I am capable of doing."

The position as court composer for Emperor Joseph II did not bring in enough to ease Mozart's burden. Neither did the success of his two operas in Prague free him from debt. He still had to give piano lessons, play at receptions, and give concerts.

He and Constanze were continually plagued by money troubles. He was not a good businessman. He was modest and retiring and lacked aggressiveness and commercial shrewdness. He had a good heart and was not suspicious of his fellow men. Because of this he was easily imposed upon. And he never succeeded in securing from music publishers and impresarios a fair share of the profits from his work.

Money earned was used to pay back debts. There was never enough left over to set aside a small reserve for illness or other emergencies. Still, regardless of his debts and the pressure of insecurity, he helped other musicians who were in greater difficulties than he.

Mozart himself was often forced to appeal to a wealthy friend, Michael Puchberg. Puchberg was a Viennese merchant, an amateur musician, and one of his brothers in Freemasonry. Many pathetic letters of appeal survive. They start with the salutation "My dear Esteemed friend and Order Brother." And they contain such phrases as "a loan of one or two thousand gulden," "with your aid I will free myself of my most pressing debts," "I will work with a mind free from care and with a lighter heart and thus be able to earn more."

Mozart's failures, his debts, and his extreme insecurity preyed heavily upon him. Yet the creative force within him overpowered all these demons. His soul remained free and his spirit unhampered.

In the summer months of 1788, following the dismal failure of *Don Giovanni* in Vienna, he wrote his three last and most famous symphonies. These three, which are numbered 39, 40, and 41, were all written in a single summer! To this day they endure as great treasures in our musical heritage. Each is different in mood, yet a perfect example of symphonic art.

The first, the symphony in E-Flat Major, No. 39, has been described as a work in which "love and melancholy breathe forth in purest spirit tones; we feel ourselves drawn with inexpressible longing toward the forms which beckon as the clouds to another sphere."

The second, the G-Minor, No. 40, has been described as a symphony "of pain, lamentation, and sorrow which rises to a climax of wide merriment." In this way does courage overcome the difficulties of life. When Richard Wagner heard this symphony for the first time it was badly played by a poor orchestra, yet he said that the music contained such great beauty that even bad musicians were unable to obscure its qualities. This symphony has often been pointed to as a clear example of those great qualities in Mozart: his glowing radiance and his sun-god temperament.

The last symphony, written in C-Major, No. 41, has been named the *Jupiter* symphony. Robert Schumann said of this work: "There are certain things in the world about which nothing can be said, such as Mozart's C-Major symphony, much of Shakespeare, and pages of Beethoven." In this last symphony, the last Mozart ever wrote, we discover that wonderful affirmation of the undying spirit of man. The stirring climax of the *Jupiter* announces to the world that man's spirit triumphs over all earthly difficulties. Hope and courage make man's spirit free; it cannot be tied to a sordid earth.

These last three symphonies, besides reaching tremendous musical heights, also marked an historic moment. They broke down the rigid conventions of the day which governed symphonic form. And they foreshadowed and paved the way for the coming of Beethoven and the liberation of music.

In the spring of the following year, 1789, Mozart enjoyed a welcome change from troubles and work in Vienna. His pupil Prince Lichnowsky, the Countess Thun's son-in-law, offered to take him in by comfortable carriage to Berlin where he would be introduced to King Frederick William II of Prussia. Mozart accepted in the hope that he might find a better position at the Prussian court or at least a profitable commission.

They set off in March and traveled leisurely, making several stops on the way. The swaying coach, the sound of the horses' hoofs, the moving landscape brought back memories. How often had Mozart and his father and mother and Nannerl traveled through Europe searching for fame and fortune. Perhaps this time he would find the long-sought-for patron. Not one like Emperor Joseph II, who paid him only a miserable wage and forced him to write minuets and waltzes.

Prince Lichnowsky and Mozart stopped first in Prague, where they spent a few days and where Mozart discussed the possibility of doing another opera. However, nothing came of this idea.

In Dresden, Mozart played before the court and was rewarded with a snuff-box containing one hundred ducats. In Leipzig, he played on the church organ of the late Johann Sebastian Bach, and there were some who thought the old master had returned to his organ bench. Here in the organ loft, Mozart was shown some of Bach's manuscripts and heard the choir sing some of his immortal hymns. These works had not yet been discovered, having been played only in this church in Leipzig. The great bulk of Bach's music was not published until almost a hundred years after his death.

Mozart was particularly pleased with this visit to Leipzig because he had long admired Bach. Many years before he had recognized and played a collection of Bach's fugues in Vienna. Besides, this Johann Sebastian Bach had been the father of the Bach whom Mozart had known as a child in London.

Arriving in Berlin, Mozart was given a friendly welcome by the Prussian King. Frederick William II was an amateur musician who had long ago heard of Mozart and his music and was eager to impress his visitor with the cultural accomplishments of his court.

At the first opportunity the King ordered his private orchestra to play for Mozart and invited him to join in their rehearsals. He was very proud of his musicians and was eager to know Mozart's opinion of them. Mozart was bold enough to say that while a number of them were very accomplished, they would produce better results if they would keep together and play in time. This was a very frank statement, but Frederick William saw the justice of the criticism and was not offended.

Mozart's visit to Berlin was a pleasant one in spite of the fact that it was filled with disappointments. Although Frederick William was very friendly, he did not offer Mozart a position at his court. Also, he was rather possessive. He would not allow Mozart to give a public concert, selfishly monopolizing the celebrated musician for himself and his friends.

Before Mozart left Berlin, however, Frederick William showed a little more generosity, and commissioned him to write six quartets and a set of easy pianoforte sonatas. Mozart was delighted, and returned to Vienna in a happy mood.

To add to Mozart's good spirits at this time, Emperor Joseph II commissioned him to write an opera around a story which he himself suggested. The plot was based on a comic episode which had just taken place in Viennese society. The title chosen was *Così fan tutte* or *The School for Lovers*. Mozart set to work at once with his librettist, Da Ponte.

His happiness, however, did not last long. Constanze was ill and needed doctors and medicines. The little money Mozart had brought home from Berlin and the two hundred ducats which the Emperor had given him were soon gone. He was again forced to apply to his merchant friend and fellow mason, Michael Puchberg, for assistance. But the aid he received was not enough, and he was so beset with worries that his usual buoyant spirits disappeared.

On top of this, musical Vienna seemed to grow more indifferent. The novelty of Mozart's unusual and sensitive piano playing, which in the past had attracted people to his concerts, had now worn off. His pupils fell away. Only two or three remained. He was only thirty-four, but he felt he was through. He sank into a state of depression and, strangely for him, he seemed unable to break through this gloom.

The result was that for the first time in his creative life he fell into a semi-barren period. The few compositions he produced, immediately after completing *Così fan tutte*, are not equal to his usual work. They clearly reflect his troubled spirit, his distraught and worried mind. His glowing spirit and his sun-god radiance had left him. Insecurity and want had driven them off.

To make matters worse, when *Così fan tutte* was produced, on January 20, 1790, it was not well received. The public did not appreciate the delicate, enchanting music.

Then to add to Mozart's bad luck, Emperor Joseph II died in March, 1790. His successor, Leopold II, cared very little for music.

Nevertheless, two months after the new Emperor had come to the throne, Mozart applied for extra work, a second position at the court. He asked the Archduke Francis, whom he knew, to present his "humble petition" to his Majesty. In this he said that "Desire of fame, love of work and the conviction of my capabilities all make me bold enough to apply for a second situation." He wanted to compose church music for the court. And should this fail he asked that he might be appointed musical instructor to the Royal Family. "The reputation I enjoy in the world for my pianoforte playing makes me venture to solicit this honor."

Unfortunately, this appeal to the new monarch produced no result. Mozart was forced once more to apply to his brother mason for a loan. In this letter he closes with the words: "My dear kind friend and brother, please do not let my begging deprive me of your friendship, and do not desert me. I rely entirely on you and am ever your most grateful Mozart. P.S. I have now only two pupils. I should like to have eight. So please endeavor to let it be known that I do not object to giving lessons."

In September of this same year Mozart saw a chance to earn a little money by going to Frankfort, where all society would be gathered for the coronation of the new Emperor, Leopold II. The French Revolution that had taken place the year before had not at all dampened the spirits of the Austrian aristocrats. They were determined to hold gala festivities to celebrate the crowning of their new Emperor. And

Mozart was quick to grasp the opportunity in the hope of relieving his desperate financial plight.

To finance this journey, Mozart pawned some household silver and a few of the valuable presents he had received from royalty. He then joined his brother-in-law, a violinist even worse off than he himself, and together they went to Frankfort.

As soon as Mozart arrived in Frankfort he wrote to his wife: "I am quite determined to do the best I can for myself here and shall then be heartily glad to return to you. What a delightful life we shall lead! I will work, and work in such a manner that I may never again be placed in so distressing a position."

He tried to keep his letters happy and hopeful, but his heart was sad and lonely. Some of the pages were blotted with tears.

In Frankfort Mozart did manage, however, to give a concert of his own music. He played two piano concertos with an orchestra, one of which the D-Major, has since been named the *Coronation* concerto. This title is misleading, for the work was not composed for Leopold's coronation but rather written by Mozart three years before. It is a happy work and quite "Mozartean."

In the composition of piano concertos, Mozart reached the greatest musical heights. His twenty-seven piano concertos can be said to be his most characteristic creations and to this day a great number of them remain undisputed masterpieces. In these compositions Mozart achieves a perfect blending of orchestra with a solo instrument, and in this fusion he expresses the deepest emotions and most profound thoughts. Yet there is always a sun-god brightness contrasted against darkness. They transport the listener into a higher world.

Following the concert in Frankfort, Mozart wrote Constanze: "It was a splendid success from the point of view of honor and glory, but a failure as far as money was concerned."

After the coronation, Mozart went to the city of Offenbach where he tried to interest the music publisher, André, in his works. But André, at this time, did not care to publish any Mozart music, in which he claimed to see no great merit.

Mozart then went on to Mannheim, where, over twenty years before, he had heard Prince Carl Theodor's great orchestra for the first time. *Figaro* was being produced at the opera house, and he wanted to help with the rehearsals. This he did. But when he tried to enter the theater on the opening night the doorman stopped him, thinking this was some little tailor trying to get in without a ticket. And he would not let the great musician pass until he had been identified.

Mozart journeyed home to Vienna by way of Heidelberg and Munich. He had set out with great hopes of freeing himself from debt and anxiety. By this trip he had hoped to buy the freedom that would permit him to continue composing. But alas, the entire venture was a failure and he was now even more deeply in debt than before!

Poverty and her companions, Anxiety and Illness, now had him so tightly in their grip that he could not shake himself free. When the Director of the Italian opera in London proposed that Mozart should come to England for six months, during which time he was to write two operas, he refused the offer. Not even a guarantee of three hundred pounds sterling (fifteen hundred dollars) and the agreement that he would be free, in London, to earn extra money by giving concerts, could tempt him. The good offer came too late. Constanze was still ill. They were so deeply in debt that Mozart felt he would not be able to raise enough money to make the trip. Besides, he had been left so crushed by the failure of his Frankfort trip that he did not have the spirit to go out into the world again at this time. He felt it was much easier just to stay at home.

Another promise was held out to Mozart at this time. In December, 1790, an English impresario, whose name was Salomon, came to Vienna and persuaded Joseph Haydn to journey to London to write some symphonies for his subscription concerts. He further proposed that Mozart should follow Haydn to London a few months later and also write some orchestral music for the same organization.

Although Mozart had refused the first offer and although he did not definitely know whether he would be able to accept the second, he nevertheless now began to rise out of his depression. It was comforting to know that somewhere in this world there were people who wanted him.

London had been kind to him in his childhood. His memories of London were still warm in his heart. And now. . . .

He determined to get back to work. Through work he would forget his difficulties. Through work he would rise again.

And so he bid farewell to his dear friend Haydn, who was leaving for London. The two spoke of plans for the future, of being together once more.

But these things were not to happen. Mozart and Haydn were never to see each other again.

The Closing Year

During 1791, the closing year of Mozart' short life, inspiration returned to him in full force.

In the month of January alone he wrote a piano concerto, three songs, and a set of four dances. And in the months that followed he wrote twelve other compositions in addition to two immortal works: the opera *The Magic Flute* and his *Requiem Mass*.

The Magic Flute had a curious origin. The idea for this opera came from Schikaneder, an actor-manager who was a friend of the Mozarts'.

Schikaneder was a man of many roles. He was born in poverty, grew up without education, became a strolling fiddler, then an actor, and finally a theatrical manager. He was shrewd, quick-witted, and ambitious. He knew his public and what they wanted.

He had rented an old barnlike theater on the outskirts of Vienna, and here he put on plays. He produced Shakespeare, Schiller, and Lessing. But his most successful plays were popular comic presentations in which drama, fantasy, and spectacle were intermingled.

After some experimenting, Schikaneder found that he could draw unusually large audiences with romantic fairy-tales set to music. He found that the public loved to see animals on the stage and that they also loved strange and fantastic scenery.

And so it was that in March of the year 1791 Schikaneder approached his friend and fellow mason, Mozart, with a proposal. He suggested that they work together on a "magic" opera that would include all three elements which he knew pleased the public. Schikaneder promised to provide the libretto and asked Mozart to compose the music. It was agreed.

Since delicate Constanze was expecting another baby and had gone to Baden to take the "baths" and breathe fresh country air, Schikaneder provided Mozart with a little summerhouse in the courtyard of his theater. Here Mozart could work undisturbed and be close at hand in case changes were needed in the libretto. And many changes were needed before the opera was half finished.

The plot which they first devised for *The Magic Flute* was quite simple. The beautiful daughter of a good fairy queen had been kidnapped and a handsome young prince went out in search of her. Before he left, the fairy queen gave him a magic silver flute which had the power to protect him from all danger. The young prince had many adventures, but finally succeeded in bringing back the queen's lost daughter.

This story was a simple one, but the further Mozart and Schikaneder proceeded with the opera, the more complicated it became. In the end the good fairy queen became a villainess and was named the Queen of the Night. And since both composer and librettist were ardent Freemasons they added many masonic rituals, including some Egyptian mysteries. Here and there, between comic situations, they sprinkled the high moral ideals of masonic philosophy. One scene takes place in an Egyptian temple, another near the pyramids, and still another in "The temple of the Sun."

The material, which was extremely fantastic, dealt in part with the mysteries of life and death. It would have seemed from the outset to be doomed to failure. But this did not turn out to be so.

During the summer of 1791 the question of life and death seemed to prey on Mozart's mind. He had a strange feeling that his earthly life was coming to an end. He was still young. He was only thirty-five. Yet he was unable to throw off the growing conviction that death was near.

And while life and death were uppermost in his

mind, in the month of July, a stranger knocked on his door. The man was tall, thin, and serious. He was dressed from head to foot in dark gray, and everything about him, his expression and his manner, seemed weird. Was this mysterious visitor a messenger sent from another world?

The stranger held a letter in his hand. This he gave to Mozart. It was from a patron who begged to remain anonymous. It complimented Mozart on his accomplishments as an artist and asked him to name a fee for composing a *Requiem*, a Mass for the dead. It also asked him to state the shortest possible time he would require to complete such a composition.

Mozart's work on *The Magic Flute* was still not finished, but it was all well in hand, and since he had long been wanting to show the new Emperor, Leopold II, that he had great ability as a composer of church music, he accepted the mysterious commission without hesitation. He was also pleased because the commission clearly stated that he would be allowed full freedom to compose this *Requiem* according to his own ideas. Only one condition was made. Under no circumstances should Mozart seek to discover the identity of his mysterious patron.

It was all very puzzling. And when the stranger dressed in gray had left, Mozart began to brood over his visit. How strange! How odd! Why, just when he was thinking of death, should a messenger in gray arrive with an offer for him to write a Mass for the dead, a *Requiem?* Was this visitor truly mortal or was he a heavenly angel in disguise? And for whom was this *Requiem Mass?* Was it not for himself, for his own death?

The stranger's visit made a deep impression upon Mozart. Again and again he tried to brush it aside, but the memory of it haunted him.

Mozart read all sorts of things into the visit of the man in gray. His nerves were on edge.

The true facts were very simple. The mysterious stranger dressed in gray was the steward of the wealthy Count Walsegg, an amateur musician who was in the habit of ordering pieces from professional composers which he passed off as his own. Now, due to the recent death of his Countess, he was asking Mozart to write a *Requiem.* This *Requiem* he planned to have performed as though it were his own composition!

Mozart missed Constanze who, because of her health, still remained in Baden where a baby boy had been born to them. Mozart had not yet seen the child, and looked forward to his wife's return in a few weeks. He wrote her that he was sad and his days tedious. "My work does not make me happy, accustomed as I am till now to pause during my labors and exchange a few words with you, but this is now impossible. If I go to the piano to begin something out of the opera it somehow affects me too much and I must stop playing."

The Magic Flute was not yet finished when he began writing out sections of the *Requiem*. Suddenly, a third important commission arrived to interrupt everything.

The Emperor Leopold II was to be crowned in Prague during the first week in September. And the people of Prague, who were ever loyal admirers of Mozart, wanted him to do an opera in honor of this occasion. It was already August. Time was pressing.

A libretto was quickly chosen and Mozart put aside the *Requiem* and *The Magic Flute* and started composing at white heat an opera called *The Clemency of Titus*. It was a pompous and frigid drama not well suited to Mozart's style, but it had been chosen because European royalty always called upon Roman history to embellish their festivities.

Mozart, together with Constanze and one of his most talented pupils, Süssmayr, set off at once for Prague. All during the journey, in the carriage and in the inns where they spent the nights, Mozart wrote out music for *The Clemency of Titus*, while Süssmayr filled in the harmonies and counterpoint.

At the end of eighteen days the opera was finished and put into rehearsal! Everything was ready for the gala performance that took place immediately after the coronation banquet.

But *The Clemency of Titus* was not a success. Mozart was too harried to achieve his best work, and while there is a good deal of fine music in this opera, it is not equal to Mozart's best. The conditions under which it was written were not conducive to good work.

Mozart was not well while he was in Prague. He was constantly taking medicines. And the mysterious stranger in gray was ever in his mind. Just before he had left Vienna for Prague the stranger had again knocked on his door with urgent inquiries as to the progress of the promised *Requiem*.

Returning to Vienna, Mozart set to work at once to finish *The Magic Flute*. Some of the chorus music was written early in September and the overture and march of the priests two days before the curtain went up on the opening performance on September thirtieth.

The Magic Flute was an immediate success. Because of its strange situations, its whole-hearted fun, comic scenes, mystery, and originality, this opera became a favorite from the very start. Recently it has again become a repertory piece in many opera houses.

Beethoven regarded *The Magic Flute* as the very best of Mozart's works, not only because of its original plot and lofty moral sentiments but also because it contained the greatest variety of musical expression. Goethe also held this opera in great esteem; some years later when he was director of the Weimar Theater he had this opera performed eighty-two times! He even dreamed of some day writing a sequel.

The captivating quality of *The Magic Flute* is that it lifts us out of the world of reality and carries us far into the world of the imagination, where the mysteries of life and death are explained in simple terms. The exalted music makes clear the deeper meanings which words alone could never convey.

The tremendous success of *The Magic Flute* was very gratifying to Mozart, but he could not free himself from his obsession with death. Returning to his work on the *Requiem* he felt certain that he was writing the Mass for his own funeral.

His tortured mind is revealed by a letter which he wrote to a friend in London during this period:

"I wish I could follow your advice but how am I able to do so? My head is confused, I reason with difficulty. Before my eyes I constantly see the image of the stranger who is ever urging me on and impatiently demanding the finished work. And I work on because composition tires me less than resting. Besides, I have nothing to fear. I know from my inner feeling that the hour must soon come. I am on the point of dying. I will finish before I can enjoy my talent. Life was so beautiful, my career began under such brilliant circumstances, but nobody is able to change his destiny. And no one is able to count his days. One must resign oneself, for it will all be as Providence desires. And so I must finish my funeral song. I must not leave it unfinished."

Mozart felt his life-forces leaving him. He felt himself doomed. Morbid ideas filled his mind. The mysterious stranger in gray he was now certain was the Angel of Death.

In October, when Constanze returned from Baden where she had again gone seeking her health, she found Mozart in a serious condition. He was almost too weak to work and she urged him to put the *Requiem* aside and rest. But his brain was heavily charged with this most serious and exalted music. He could not rest. He could not stop. Death was overpowering. Death was imminent. And he was writing his funeral song.

In the following month, November, he felt a little better and put aside the very serious music of the *Requiem* to write some music for a festival being planned by his masonic lodge. He composed a cantata, and on the fifteenth of the month was well enough to conduct the performance.

Two days later he suffered a serious relapse of weakness and depression. He tried to fight it off. He even made the effort of visiting a café, the *Silver*

Serpent, which was close by his home. This was a place where authors, singers, and musicians gathered, and here Mozart was well known.

On this day, it is recorded, Mozart entered the café and dropped exhausted into a chair. Leaning against the table he rested his head in his hands and remained in this position for a long time. Without moving, he ordered the waiter to bring him a glass of wine, although he usually drank beer. And even after the wine had been set before him he did not move, did not even taste it.

At this point Joseph Deiner, Mozart's friend and steward of the *Silver Serpent*, came into the room.

Mozart looked up and said: "Well, Joseph, how are things?"

"I ought to ask you that. You look sick and miserable, Maestro. You're drinking wine now, and that's a good idea, because I suppose the beer you had in Prague must have spoiled your stomach. It's nothing serious, Maestro!"

"My stomach is better than you think. I've learned to swallow all sorts of things." When he spoke these words Mozart sighed.

"All sickness begins in the stomach," said Deiner, seating himself at his friend's table.

"There's a chill that has come over me and I can't understand it. Here, Deiner, drink up this wine for me. Come to the house tomorrow morning. Winter is setting in and we will need wood for our fires. My wife will go with you to buy the wood. I'm even having a fire made up today."

Mozart then called the waiter, pressed a coin in his hand, and left the tavern.

The next morning Joseph Deiner, according to his account, walked over to Mozart's apartment to see about the firewood. On the way he recalled how the year before he had also visited the Mozarts and how the question of firewood had come up. At that time he had found Mozart and his wife dancing wildly around the room.

Deiner had asked Mozart if he was teaching his wife dancing and Mozart had laughed and said: "No, of course not. We are only warming ourselves. We are freezing and we can't buy any wood." Deiner had then gone home and brought Mozart some of his own wood which Mozart later repaid.

But on this morning when Deiner came to Mozart's apartment he did not find his friend dancing. The maid who answered the door said: "We had to call the doctor during the night because the Maestro was very sick."

Going into Mozart's room and standing beside Constanze, Deiner gazed down at his friend lying in bed with his eyes closed. Mozart was very pale and still, but sensing that his friend Deiner was near he opened his eyes and said in a very weak voice:

"There is nothing doing today, Joseph, just doctors and druggists."

In bed or out of it, day after day Mozart kept on working on parts of the *Requiem*. The urgency to finish it seemed to keep him from death.

Sometimes he would dictate what he had in mind to his able pupil, Süssmayr. At other times he showed Süssmayr the melodic line of a section that was still to come and which he had quickly sketched in on music paper. He also indicated how he intended to fill in the various parts. It was almost as though he feared that he would not live long enough to complete this work. It was almost as though he wanted someone else to know exactly what he intended.

He was completely absorbed by the *Requiem*, yet when evening came he would watch the time closely. In his imagination he followed the performances of *The Magic Flute*, which was playing to crowded houses in another section of Vienna.

"Now," he would say, looking at his watch. "Now it is time. The orchestra is beginning to play the overture." At any moment he could tell, by looking at his watch, exactly what was being sung on the stage.

"Now we are at the end of the act," he would announce. Or: "Now comes the grand aria for the Queen of the Night."

Night after night *The Magic Flute* played to immense crowds. Schikaneder collected a small fortune from this success, but the dying Mozart had already been paid in full. He had received a small sum outright and while he shared in the glory of the success he had no share in the profits.

At the end of November, several doctors were called into consultation. Due to his swollen limbs, it was difficult for Mozart to leave his bed. But the doctors were of little help. They were not able to diagnose his trouble.

During the first days of December the doctors were again called. But what good were they against exhaustion and a heart broken by poverty and humiliation? For this condition they had no medicine, but they wrote out prescriptions anyway. And while they were about it they wrote out another for Constanze. She, too, needed medicine.

On the fourth of December Mozart remarked that he would like to hear some of the parts of his unfinished *Requiem*. He was confined to his bed and very ill, but Constanze asked four of his friends, musicians, to come in and try some of the music. However, before they had played and sung very long, Mozart asked them to stop. He was too weak. And he then realized that he could not live long enough to finish the work. Tears came to his eyes.

Turning to Constanze he said: "I have the taste of death on my tongue. I know now that I am writing the *Requiem* for myself. But before I go I wish I could hear once again my *Magic Flute*." Then in a small weak voice he began singing the bird-catcher's song from this opera. And one of his friends went to the piano and accompanied him.

The next night, Süssmayr sat up with him until midnight. Melodies were ringing in Mozart's mind. Suddenly he leaned his head against the wall, closed his eyes and fell asleep. A short time later life passed from him. It was December 5, 1791.

A funeral service arranged by Baron van Swieten was held at St. Stephen's Church on the following day. A few friends were present, but Constanze was too ill to attend.

The weather was dark and stormy. Sleet and snow were falling. His friends started out in the storm to follow the coffin to the cemetery, but the weather grew worse and they turned back at the city wall.

He was buried in a common grave. No friend or relative was present to see the coffin lowered into the ground. And a few days later there was no one who could point to the place which contained the remains of Wolfgang Amadeus Mozart.

All attempts to discover the exact spot where Mozart was buried have failed. His grave remains unmarked.

His monument is his music.

And After

As soon as it was known in Vienna that Mozart was dead, the mysterious stranger in gray again knocked on the door. He now frankly revealed himself as the servant of Count Walsegg. Where was the *Requiem?*

A good part of the *Requiem* was finished. Mozart had completed all the early sections and the score was as perfectly finished and as beautiful as anything he had ever composed. A few numbers, however, remained to be done. These Mozart had already outlined, and these his pupil Süssmayr undertook to complete. In a very short time the full score was delivered to Count Walsegg. And, as he had planned, the Count had the work performed as his own.

But some time later he relented and admitted that the *Requiem* was Mozart's work.

However, when Constanze, who had been left destitute with two small children, gave the manuscript to a music publisher, the Count protested. He said the *Requiem* belonged to him because he had ordered it written and had paid for it. He threatened Constanze with a lawsuit, but he changed his mind and dropped the case. And he even allowed his original copy to be used in revising the publisher's proofs.

Thus ended the strange story—strange as any in the history of music—of Mozart's last work, the *Requiem*.

Mozart left books and music which the assessors valued at twenty-three florins, or less than ten dollars in our money. His debts amounted to three thousand florins. And his apartment was described by a visitor as "simple and poverty-stricken."

During Mozart's lifetime, only about seventy of his compositions had been published. Although many of his works were in circulation in manuscript copies, many others existed only in the original copies left in his own papers. After his death, Constanze did not realize for some time the potential value of this musical property. The papers were in a state of hopeless confusion, and she did not have the ability to sort them out herself. In 1792, she did sell eight manuscripts to the King of Prussia, Frederick William II, for eight hundred ducats, or about fifteen hundred dollars, but for several years afterwards, little further attention was paid to the papers.

Finally, in 1798, the publishers Breitkopf & Härtel of Leipzig sensed a coming Mozart boom, and announced plans to publish a collected edition of Mozart's compositions. They asked Constanze for help. Constanze then took steps to have the papers sorted. She enlisted the aid of an old friend of Mozart's, the Abbé Maximilian Stadler, who was a fine musician and scholar, and who prepared a thorough catalogue.

While Constanze was negotiating with Breitkopf & Härtel, there suddenly appeared on the scene a young music publisher, Johann Anton André of Offenbach. André understood the value of the papers, and when he learned that they might be for sale, he quickly came to terms with Constanze and, in 1799, purchased from her all of Mozart's compositions still in her possession.

André took great pride in his collection and added to it when he could during his lifetime. He tried to preserve it as a whole, but the German government refused to purchase it. André's heirs finally started to sell it piecemeal. The Prussian government then purchased the greater part of it; but today important autographs by Mozart are also to be found in many libraries throughout Europe and America.

Most of Mozart's unpublished compositions were

printed during the nineteenth century, and finally Breitkopf & Härtel, who had become the most important German music publisher, did bring out a great collected edition of nearly all of Mozart's compositions between 1877 and 1883. A new collected edition is today being prepared in Germany.

The shock of Mozart's death seems to have had a transforming effect on Constanze. She opened a rooming house and eventually, in 1809, married the Danish Consul, Georg Nikolaus von Nissen, who was one of her roomers. Through her he became interested in Mozart, and when he retired in 1820, they moved to Salzburg where he did research and wrote the first biography of the great composer.

Constanze was a good mother to her two boys, Mozart's sons, and they grew up to be fine men, but neither of them inherited a single spark of their father's divine fire.

Constanze lived for half-a-century after Mozart's death. Year by year during this half-century she had the satisfaction of seeing his fame mount higher and higher.

However, one of his greatest tributes came only a few weeks after his death. Joseph Haydn, returning from London, wrote to a friend: "I am childishly glad to be home and welcomed by my old friends. I only regret and miss the greeting of the great Mozart, whose death I deplore. Posterity will not see such a talent for a century to come."

A Note about the Köchel Listing

Since the vast number of compositions left by Mozart contained no opus numbers it was difficult to identify them or to know their chronological order. Ludwig von Köchel, an Austrian naturalist and musician, took upon himself the task of giving each composition a number and arranging these in chronological order.

To accomplish this gigantic task he examined Mozart's letters, concert programs, newspaper items, and even the ink and paper of the manuscripts. The result was the Köchel catalogue, which was first published in 1862, seventy-one years after Mozart's death.

Since that time Mozart's compositions have been marked with the Köchel number. The letter K stands for Köchel. Thus we find that K. 1 is a Minuet and and Trio for Piano, and Mozart's first work, while his last work, the *Requiem*, has the listing of K. 626.

Many of the K. numbers include a group of compositions, as Six Minuets for Orchestra (K. 599), or Six German Dances (K. 600), or a complete opera containing over thirty numbers such as *The Magic Flute* (K. 620). Therefore it would be wrong to conclude that Mozart wrote only 626 compositions, as indicated by the highest K. number. Mozart wrote very close to a thousand compositions.

The K. numbers have been fairly accurate, but in recent years the Köchel listing has been revised and made more complete by the scholarship of the distinguished German musicologist Alfred Einstein. This new revised K. listing is today the one attached to all Mozart compositions.

Index

Abduction from the Seraglio, The, 112–13
Abel, Carl Frederick, 37, 43–4
Allegri, Gregorio, 64; *see also Miserere*
André, Johann, 149
André, Johann Anton, 169
Arabian Nights, The, 50

Bach, Johann Christian, 37, 43–4, 145
Bach, Johann Sebastian, 37, 111–12, 145
Baden, 154, 157, 161
Bastien and Bastienne, 58
Bavaria, 103–4
Beaumarchais, Caron de, 127
Beethoven, Ludwig van, 111, 122, 136, 143–4, 159
Berlin, 31, 144–6
Bologna Philharmonic Society, 69
Breitkopf & Härtel, 169, 170
British Museum, 43
Brussels, 31–2
Bullinger, Abbé Joseph, 92

Carl Theodor, Prince, 84–6, 97, 150
Clemency of Titus, The, 158
Clementi, Muzio, 113–14
Coronation Concerto, 149
Cosí fan tutte, 146–7

Da Ponte, Lorenzo, 126–8, 133, 135, 146
Deiner, Joseph, 162–4
Don Giovanni, 118, 133, 135–9, 142
Dresden, 144

Eine kleine Nachtmusik, 135
Einstein, Alfred, 172
Esterhazy, Prince Nicalaus, 123, 133

Francis, Archduke, 147
Frankfort, 29–31, 148–51
Frederick the Great, 31
Frederick William II of Prussia, 144–6, 169
French Revolution, 25, 127, 148

i

Index

Galitzin, Prince, 111
George III, 36, 38–9, 42
Gluck, Christoph Willibald, 68, 140–1
Goethe, Johann Wolfgang, 31, 159–60

Hagenauer, Lorenz, 20, 22
Handel, George Frederick, 36–9, 44, 111
Haydn, Joseph, 77–8, 123–5, 133–4, 151–2, 169
Heidelberg, 28, 150
Holland, 44–5

Idomeneo, 103–4
Italy, 61–2, 72

Joseph II, Emperor, 112–14, 127–8, 140–1, 146–7
Jupiter Symphony, 143

Kelly, Michael, 128–9
Köchel, Ludwig von, catalogues Mozart's compositions, 171–2

Lange, Josef, 101, 114; *see also* Aloysia Weber
Lange, Aloysia, *see* Aloysia Weber
Leipzig, 145
Leopold II, Emperor, 147–9, 156, 158

Leopold, Grand Duke of Tuscany, 76
Lessing, Gotthold Ephraim, 154
Lichnowsky, Prince Karl, 111, 144
London, 36–44, 151–2, 160, 169
Louis XV, 32, 35
Louis XVI, 34, 127–8

Magic Flute, The, 153–5, 158–60, 164, 166, 171
Mannheim, 84–6, 97, 150
Marie Antoinette, 25, 127–8
Marriage of Figaro, The, 118, 127–33, 150
Martini, Padre, 64
Mass in C Minor, 117–18
Maximilian Joseph, 19, 81–n
Mesmer, Dr. Franz Anto3 von, 58
Mesmerism, 58
Milan, Opera house, 70–1, 75
Miserere (Allegri), 64–5
Mithridates, King of Pontus, 70
Mozart, Anna Maria (*Mozart's mother*), 3, 8, 69, 80, 92
Mozart, Carl (*Mozart's son*), 130
Mozart, Constanze (*Mozart's wife*, neé Weber), 114–18, 154, 157–8, 165–6, 168–70

Index

Mozart, Leopold (*Mozart's father*), 6–7, 11, 14–15, 83, 86–92; son's rebellion against, 100, 105–7, 117, 119, 130; *Violin Method* of, 14, 45, 94

Mozart, Maria Ann (Nannerl) (*Mozart's sister*), 8, 10, 26–7, 41, 66–9

Mozart, Wolfgang Amadeus: birth and baptism, 3–4; parentage, 6–8; musical sensibility, 9–10; musical education, 10–11; first compositions, 11–13; receives first violin, 15–17; trip to Munich, 18–19; first journey to Vienna, 20–2; plays for the Empress Maria Theresa, 23–4; ill with scarlet fever, 25; continues musical education, 26–7; leaves on "grand tour," 28; plays his first organ, 28; appearance in Frankfort, 29–31; visits French court, 33–4; hears French music, 35; visits London, 36; meets Johann Christian Bach, 37; plays for King George III, 38–9; composes first symphony, 41–2; falls ill in Holland, 45; musical inspiration, 47; composes oratorio, 49;

Mozart, Wolfgang Amadeus (*continued*)
schooling and education, 50–1; ill with smallpox, 53; royal concert in Vienna, 54; commissioned to write first opera, 56–7; writes *Bastien and Bastienne* for Dr. Mesmer, 58; appointed Kapellmeister, 59–60; first trip to Italy, 61; commissioned to write opera for Milan Opera house, 64; writes down *Miserere* from memory, 64–6; letter to his sister, 67; receives *Order of the Golden Spur* from the Pope, 68; voted a member of the Academy of Bologna, 69; conducts opera *Mithridates, King of Pontus*, 70; returns to Salzburg, 72; second trip to Milan to compose serenade for wedding of Archduke Ferdinand, 72–73; dissatisfied under new Archbishop, 74–5; returns to Milan to rehearse new opera, 75; visit to Vienna, 76; special musical quality, 77; influence of Joseph Haydn, 77–8; seeks his fortune elsewhere, 80; meets the Elector of Ba-

iii

Mozart, Wolfgang Amadeus (*continued*)
varia, 81–3; visits Mannheim, 84–6; arrives in Paris, 89; plays for the Duchess de Bourbon, 90; mourns over his mother's death, 92; father persuades him to return to Salzburg, 93–6; concert in Strasbourg, 96; decides to visit Mannheim, 97; romance with Aloysia Weber, 98–101; difficulties working for Archbishop, 102; composes opera *Idomeneo*, 103–4; journey to Vienna with Archbishop, 104–5; resigns from Archbishop's service, 106; father's displeasure, 107–8; freedom in Vienna, 109–10; finds pupils, 110–11; composes opera *The Abduction from the Seraglio*, 112; contest with Clementi, 113–14; marriage to Constanze Weber, 114–17; composes *Mass in C Minor*, 117–18; visits Salzburg, 117–18; describes life in Vienna, 120–1; method of composition, 121–2; begins catalogue of his compositions, 123; friendship with Joseph

Mozart, Wolfgang Amadeus (*continued*)
Haydn, 123–5; meets Lorenzo da Ponte, 126–7; composes opera *The Marriage of Figaro*, 127–9; feelings of failure, 130–1; visit to Prague, 132–3; Haydn recommends as an opera composer, 133–4; composes *Eine kleine Nachtmusik*, 135; composes opera *Don Giovanni*, 135–8; meeting with Beethoven, 136; writes down Overture of *Don Giovanni* the night before the first performance, 137–38; failure of *Don Giovanni* in Vienna, 139–40; appointed court composer, 140; lack of money, 141–2; composes his last three symphonies, 142–3; journey to Berlin, 144–6; visits Dresden, 144; visits Leipzig and studies Bach's music, 145; composes opera *Così fan tutte*, 146; financial worries increase, 146–8; visit to Frankfort, 149; performs *Coronation* Concerto, 149; visits Mannheim for last time, 150; poverty increases, 151; refuses trip to

Index

Mozart, Wolfgang Amadeus (*continued*)
London, 151; composes opera *The Magic Flute*, 154–5; preoccupation with death, 155–7; commissioned to write *Requiem*, 157; despondency affects work, 157; composes opera *The Clemency of Titus*, 158; finishes *The Magic Flute*, 159; writes letter to unknown friend revealing obsession with death, 160–1; falls ill, 161–5; attempts to complete *Requiem*, 164; last visit of his friends, 165; death and burial, 166; subsequent disposition of his manuscripts, 168–70; tribute by Haydn, 170; works catalogued by Köchel, 171–2
Mozart Museum, 52
Munich, 19, 81, 98, 150
Musical education, 10, 11, 15–17

Nissen, Georg Nicolaus von, 169

Offenbach, city of, 150, 168
Olmütz, 53
Opera, 44, 69–70, 74, 121; *see also The Pretended Sim-*

Opera (*continued*)
pleton; Bastien and Bastienne; Mithridates, King of Pontus; Idomeneo; The Abduction from the Seraglio; The Marriage of Figaro; Don Giovanni; Così fan tutte; The Magic Flute; and *The Clemency of Titus*
Oratorio, juvenile, composed at Archbishop's demand, 49
Order of the Golden Spur, 68

Paris, 32–6, 88
Passau, 21
Podstatsky, Count Leopold Anton von, 53
Pompadour, Madame de, 34
Prague, 131–4, 136–9, 141, 144, 158–9
Prague Opera house, 133, 139
Prague orchestra, plays Overture of *Don Giovanni* at sight, 138
Pretended Simpleton, The, 56
Puchberg, Michael, 142, 146, 148

Requiem Mass, 153, 156–61, 164–8
Rumbeck, Countess von, 110

St. Stephen's Church, 166
Salomon, Johann Peter, 151

v

Salzburg, 4, 48–52, 72, 118
Schachtner, Johann Andreas, 11–12, 16–17
Schikaneder, Johann Emanuel, 153–5, 165
Schiller, Johann Christoph von, 154
Schumann, Robert, 143
Seven Years' War, 32
Shakespeare, William, 143, 154
Silver Serpent café, 161–2; *see also* Joseph Deiner
Six German Dances, K.600, 172
Six Minuets for Orchestra, K.599, 172
Solemn Mass, now lost, 59
Stadler, Abbé Maximilian, 169
Storace, Nancy, 128
Strasbourg, 96
Süssmayr, Franz Xaver, 158, 164, 166–7
Swieten, Baron Gottfried van, 111, 166
Symphonies no. 39, 40, and 41, 142

Symphony no. 1 in E-flat Major, 42

Thamos, King of Egypt, 103
Thun, Count Johann Joseph, 132
Thun, Countess Wilhelmine, 111–12, 132, 144

Versailles, 33–34, 91
Vienna, 22–25, 104–7, 139, 164, 167
Vienna Opera house, cabals in, 56–7, 129
Voltaire, François Marie Arouet, 87

Wagner, Richard, 143
Waldstadten, Baroness von, 111
Walsegg, Count Franz von, 157, 167–8
Weber, Aloysia, 98–101, 114–15, 140
Weber, Constanze, *see* Constanze Mozart
Weimar Theater, 159; *see also* Goethe
Wenzel, Herr, 16

A NOTE ON THE

Type

IN WHICH THIS BOOK IS SET

THE TEXT *of this book was set on the Monotype in Janson, a recutting made direct from type cast from the original matrices cut by Anton Janson. Janson, who may have been of Dutch origin, purchased a foundry and was a practicing type-founder in Leipzig between 1660 and 1687. His first specimen sheet was issued in 1675. His successor, Johann Karl Edling, issued a later specimen sheet showing all of Janson's types in 1689. The Janson matrices were later brought to Holland, from whence they were sold in 1720 to the Erhardt foundry of Leipzig. Later acquired by the Drugulin foundry of Leipzig, they eventually passed into the hands of the Schriftgiesserei Stempel of Frankfurt am Main, where they are now preserved.*

Janson is an excellent example of the sturdy and influential Dutch old style types that prevailed throughout Europe during the seventeenth and early eighteenth centuries. It is highly legible, and its individual letters have a pleasing variety of design.

THE BOOK was composed, printed, and bound by Kingsport Press, Inc., Kingsport, Tennessee. Paper manufactured by P. H. Glatfelter Co., Spring Grove, Pa. Typography by Warren Chappell.